By My Mother's Hand

As Told by Survivor Henry Melnick

By My Mother's Hand

© 2011 Henry Melnick. All rights reserved.
Story chronicled by Limore Zisckind
Afterword by Faith Dantowitz
Edited by Michael Melnick and Faith Dantowitz
Cover design by Hee Yol Lee
ISBN 978-0-557-52253-8

Table of Contents

Acknowledgements	11
Prologue	13
My First Memories	19
Growing up Jewish in the Community of Lodz	33
The Germans Invade Poland	41
Arrival in Nowy Sącz	47
The Ghetto in Nowy Sącz	57
The Nowy Sącz Ghetto Liquidation	65
The Tarnów Ghetto	73
At Szebnie Camp	81
Szebnie Liquidation	91
The Road to Auschwitz	95
Life in Auschwitz II - Birkenau	101
Auschwitz III (Buna-Monowitz)	107
The Death March to Gleiwitz II	119
Dora-Mittelbau	125
Bergen-Belsen and the End of the War	135

LIBERATION!	143
RECOVERY AT CELLE	149
HELA'S STORY	153
HELA AND HENRY IN HANOVER	165
LIFE TOGETHER AFTER THE WAR	171
A NEW LIFE IN ISRAEL	179
PRESENT DAY IN TORONTO – IN MY OWN WORDS	187
AFTERWARD	193
APPENDIX	195

This book is dedicated to and in memory of my late wife Hela (Chaya) Melnick, and all of my relatives that did not survive the war. I am the sole survivor of my entire family.

Acknowledgements

I leave my story as a legacy to my children, grandchildren and great-grandchildren to pass down for generations to come. Read, learn, grow and appreciate your lives. My story is but one of six million.

I was inspired to come forward with my testimony by remembering what my mother said to me: "Somebody must survive to tell our story."

In writing this book, my intention is not to teach hate but to teach tolerance. Intolerance left unchecked leads to stories like mine. Thank you to my wife Elaine for encouraging me to share my story and for lending her love and support.

I would like to thank my grandson Michael for his effort and dedication in his roles as editor and designer.

Also thank you to Faith Dantowitz, Elaine Melnick's daughter, for final editing.

Lastly, I want to thank my granddaughter Limore for encouraging me to write this book and spending so much time with me to chronicle and publish my words.

Prologue

Being one of Henry's seven grandchildren, I was fortunate to work on this book to pass on to the next generation. I would like to share some of my thoughts while chronicling my grandfather Henry Melnick's personal testimony.

Several years ago, while listening to my grandfather talk at a speaking engagement, a frightening thought entered my mind. What will happen when he is no longer here to share his experience? I ached to remember every detail, every word and every nuance as he spoke. How could I remember his entire history? That was when I decided to record his chronicles.

So began regularly scheduled visits to my grandfather's home. I often visited during the evenings, arriving hungry after work. Bubbie Elaine would make us dinner. Over 24 months and many bowls of soup, I listened.

While chronicling Henry's experiences, I tried to stay true to his voice. I did not embellish nor add my own feelings. I asked many questions in order to try and evoke emotion, but sometimes I felt like I could not push any further. At times I could tell it was just too painful for him.

On numerous occasions I have heard Henry speak. His fact-based style of recounting his tragic story amplifies the depth, breadth and magnitude of his loss and his experience. Only once during my interview process did I see the glimmer of tears in his eyes – when I asked about his family life before the war. Henry was used to openly talking about his experiences in the ghettos and death camps, but he rarely, if ever, spoke about family life. When asked about growing up before the war, I saw my grandfather shaking from sadness. I wished I could have asked him more about his mother, father and siblings.

He provided me with many materials to help me record his story; endless pictures, letters, books and handwritten notes. He did not want to forget anything. Henry also gave me binders and envelopes full of thank-you notes from students and educators that expressed gratitude to him after hearing his words.

I am honoured to have had the privilege of recording his story. Every word has been etched into my soul. Only through spending this precious time with him have I come to fully understand the degree of his strength, courage, resilience and kindness. Instead of lashing out at the world for the injustices he endured, my grandfather continuously preaches tolerance. It is a lesson this world is far behind in learning.

Limore (Twena) Zisckind

By My Mother's Hand

As Told by Survivor Henry Melnick

My First Memories

I have no memory of my mother's face. We look like a picture-perfect family in my only remaining family photo – my father, sister, brother and I – taken one Saturday morning in a park in Lodz, Poland. My mother missed this one perfect moment, and because of that, I no longer remember what she looks like, not even her face. So many missed moments and missed opportunities enabled my survival and forced so many others to perish.

This is the only surviving photograph of my family from before the war. It was given to me shortly after I arrived in Israel following the war. Friends of my parents from Lodz, who moved from Poland before the war had this among their family photos.

Back row left to right: Yosef (my brother), Elijah (my father)
Front row left to right: Genia (my sister), Henry (me)

I was born on June 25th, 1922 in Lodz, Poland to Chaya and Elijah Chmielnicki. My sister Genia was two years younger than I. She died when she was nine years old from a disease that no one talked about or really understood. I recall her falling ill one summer after returning from summer camp. A few weeks later she died. She may have had leukemia or kidney disease.

My brother Yosef was two years older than I. He acted like my boss and we loved each other very much. We would give our lives for each other and could not imagine being apart. I'll never forget how after playing checkers, the loser would always throw down all the pieces to the floor out of frustration.

My brother and sister were both quite studious. My sister would constantly write letters on pages. Back then, times and parents were stricter and children did not know everything that happened within the family like financial problems or political matters. Interrupting parents was never allowed and we were always careful to show respect when they spoke. I believe we were kept innocent through these rules. Today, it seems to me that children tell their parents what to do.

My father Elijah was born in a shtetl[1] near Lodz. I remember him as a thin, handsome man. He was also always preoccupied and worried about providing for our family. We grew up during the depression but somehow we never went hungry. Sometimes we even refused my mother's food.

Lodz was the largest textile manufacturing hub in Poland, second in Europe only behind Manchester, England. In Lodz, my father owned and operated a sock factory. At that time his little factory employed three or four people. My mother used to also help my father with the business working in assembly.

My mother, Chaya, loved us very much. She used to make us clothes and repair those that were damaged or torn and needed patches. Back then, our closets were pretty empty and getting a new sweater was a big deal.

---

[1] A small Jewish town or village.

My mother used to hug us all the time. My father did too, but not as much. My parents never hugged each other in front of us. This behaviour was considered unacceptable. Though they did not dress in the orthodox fashion, they were still very traditional in their behaviour. All we knew about love and marriage was that a man must love his wife. My parents did not overtly explain this to us; we understood through their actions towards each other. Whatever I learned about sex, I learned in the courtyard of our building. A boy I knew told me that he used to share a bed with his father. One night he woke up and his father was in his mother's bed…that was our sex education.

I did not know either of my grandparents because they lived in the 1800s during the epidemics of cholera and tuberculosis. They died very young, long before I was born. We never spoke of the dead so I do not even know their names nor do I have a picture. Growing up, I would always hear stories about different diseases such as cancer, which they described as a very hard illness. Medicine was not very advanced back then.

My mother had two sisters; Chana and Esther. My mother's older sister, Esther, lived with her married daughter only two blocks away. We used to visit them all the time with my mother. Esther had three children, they were all older and their names are lost to me. My mother's other sister Chana Abramovitz and my uncle, Wolf, had four children; three boys – Chaskel, Avraham, Leible, and a girl – Tzela. They were all older than us. I fondly remember that Purim[2] at Doda[3] Chana's was always a party. We would dress up in all kinds of costumes; Haman, Achashverosh and Esther.

My mother used to sing traditional Yiddish lullabies like "Oyfn Pripechik." I used to speak Polish with my mother and Yiddish with my father because he never learned proper Polish.

In our family I told my mother I always felt like I was the middle of the sandwich. My mother told me that as

---

[2] A Jewish holiday that commemorates the deliverance of the Jewish people in the ancient Persian Empire from destruction in the wake of a plot by Haman, a story recorded in the biblical Book of Esther (Megillat Esther).

[3] The Hebrew word for Aunt.

many children as she has, she loves them all equally! My brother was very active and talkative, my sister was very studious and I felt stuck in the middle. I felt like I didn't have a voice.

Our family residence was at 35 Piotrkowska Street, within the centre of Lodz in a prestigious area known as Hoyche Fentzte, which literally translates to "High Windows." It was called this because most of the buildings looked similar and they all had very tall windows.

Our apartment was small; two bedrooms, one room for my parents and one room for the three siblings. Our apartment was on the third level and had red-stained wooden floors. Every room had a ceramic oven for heat and the kitchen had a tiled ceramic stove that burned wood and coal. There was an arched gateway built into each building. After eleven o'clock at night the doors were locked and one had to pay the janitor to enter. Through the archway there was a courtyard and the building continued with entrances through the apartments with many different staircases. The bathrooms were on the ground floor, with a separate building of outhouses. The outhouses had an oven in the winter that the superintendent would ensure was lit.

In our building there were 25 apartments. On the front of our building, along Piotrkowska, there were shops and restaurants and above was our housing. The stores looked out onto Piotrkowska Street. This was a place where the Jewish military and Jewish families spent many precious moments.

Our apartment was like a train station, with frequent visits from many including my Aunt Chana who lived on the third floor within the same courtyard. Our apartment felt warm and welcoming. Our door was always open to friends and family and there were always visitors.

My mother's distant relative, Sarah, lived on the ground floor of our building where she ran a small grocery store. "Cousin" Sarah had three daughters and a son. Two of her daughters were married and lived in Lodz (I cannot recall their names). The third daughter,

Regina, got married and moved to Palestine[4] before the war (she has since passed away). Sarah's son Simon was a doctor in Lodz but didn't survive the war.

Once a year for Passover we would all get new clothes. That meant one pair of pants, a shirt and shoes and that's all. Socks would come easily because of my father's factory. All other items were in short supply. I remember breaking a glass at dinner one night and getting yelled at because it could not be replaced. I never lost anything as a child because, simply, I had no personal belongings to lose!

As a family we would go visit my uncle Itzhak, my father's brother, and his wife Genendel. They lived about a half-hour walk from our apartment. I recall going with my mother to buy kosher meat from her cousin Isaac, the butcher. He also lived nearby.

My mother was a good cook. She made excellent cholent[5]. To prepare this she had to bring it to the local

---

[4] Modern-day Israel.

[5] A traditional Jewish stew consisting of meat, potatoes, beans and barley.

bakery on Friday afternoon to put in the oven. Then, on Shabbat (Saturday) midday, we would pick it up. About 50-100 people left their cholent pots with the baker every Friday. The baker would put a sticker on the pot so we would know which one was ours. My mother used to make kasha[6], which I loved. She made it with stock gravy since we did not always have beef, and chicken was very expensive. There was a shortage of chicken then, unlike today.

On Shabbat we children would go with my father to one of the parks near our house. There, we would often have pictures taken. I recall that the children who had bikes were considered rich. We would play in the courtyard with the neighbours' kids; my best friend was Heniek Rosenberg who lived in the same complex of buildings. I only remember having Jewish friends. Our entire neighbourhood was Jewish.

Back then, unlike today, most Jewish people did not have dogs in their homes. I was frightened of dogs, as

---

[6] A traditional dish consisting of buckwheat.

were my friends. If we wandered into any of the Christian areas around town, the children would sic their dogs on us and the parents would watch laughing. Their parents were often the masterminds encouraging these vicious assaults.

When I was twelve I got my first pair of ice skates. To me that was an exciting event! We used to screw the metal blades onto my shoes. I went to the shoemaker to affix an aluminum plate to the bottom, then I would go to the local ice rink in Lodz and do kunztim, or tricks, on the ice like a performer; I thought I was very good.

My cousin Leible used to play hockey in the Bar Kochba athletics club[7]. Once, he took me along to one of his games against a non-Jewish team. We knew that if his team won, they would beat us up, and if they lost, they would still beat us up. So, we called the police when his team lost to escort us to the streetcar. Once we made it onto the streetcar and the hooligans were outside, we

---

[7] The "Bar Kochba (B.K.)/ HaKoach" Jewish athletics club of Berlin (1902) was one of many Jewish sports organizations at the turn of the century.

were safe from physical assault. We experienced a lot of anti-Semitism in Poland.

In the mornings I went to public school and in the afternoon to the Cheder[8]. I used to study Hebrew and Chumash[9] at Cheder. Cheder was orthodox and boys and girls sat separately. In first grade at school I recall wearing pants with a vest attached. The pants had buttons in the back with a flap that would come undone so when I had to go to the bathroom, I did not have to take off my whole outfit. Though I was a decent student, I enjoyed playing more than studying. I do recall the rabbi at Cheder having a whip but he never hit anyone.

I attended a large boys-only public school at which all the children were Jewish. Located in a very Jewish area, there was one non-Jewish teacher that I knew of in the entire school. My favorite subjects were history and geography. These subjects were much more interesting to me than mathematics. I enjoyed exploring all of the

---

[8] A biblical or religious school.

[9] The Five Books of Moses, or Torah (Bible).

continents, different countries and the histories of the kingdoms, world leaders and dynasties.

Growing up Jewish in the Community of Lodz

The Jewish community of Lodz had over 200,000 Jews, one-third of the Lodz population of 600,000. There was an elected Jewish community president and many Jewish organizations. Many Zionist organizations flourished in Poland including Beitar, Hashomer Hatzair, Gordonia and others. There was even a Jewish hospital we believed was supported by and named after the Poznański family.

Mr. Poznański was once the leader of the Jewish community. A very rich industrialist, Israel Poznański died in 1900. His descendants disappeared during the holocaust. The Poznański family built themselves several castles around Poland, their largest castle being in Lodz. The family lived in the castle until the end of the Golden Era, after World War I. The Poznański family legacy remains through their palatial estate in Lodz, now the Lodz Museum, and their family mausoleum, built on the land Poznański purchased and donated to the community for a Jewish cemetery.

Jews actively served in the Polish army and were good citizens of Poland. Still, the Polish government was anti-Semitic and would not allow Jews to work in most public jobs like policemen, firemen or in government offices; a Jew could not even be a government janitor! We could die for their country but we could not be a part of government. For most Jews it was a constant struggle just to make a living.

There were regular performances at the Yiddish theatre from time to time, but I do not remember attending. My parents would share the details of performers such as Dzigan and Schumacher, both Yiddish comedians. These talented artists survived the war in

Russia and I actually got to see them later in life in Toronto. Half a block away in every direction from our apartment there were movie theatres. I used to enjoy watching Al Jolson in The Jazz Singer. Sometimes they showed Yiddish movies; my favorite actor was Moishe Oysher, a talented Yiddish actor and singer.

There were many stores in and around our neighbourhood. At the entrance of our building there was a gate that a horse and wagon could pass through, and in the courtyard were many thriving businesses; textile stores, printing shops, carpenter shops and bakeries. The Kosher restaurant in our development was very popular with Jewish soldiers. Many of the Jewish soldiers stationed in town; four regiments totaling one hundred Jews, would come and eat in our building during the holidays. All the children of our community had a good time with them; we would laugh together, share stories and sing Jewish Polish songs. We loved it when the soldiers sang.

We did not have many toys growing up, unlike today's children who have a million toys but end up playing with pots and pans. We were happy playing simple games like "Five Stones" with a little ball. Life was much simpler. We used to drink coffee and I loved having "cacao"-chocolate milk.

During the war, in Auschwitz and Buna, I often thought back about these treats and together with other prisoners, we would recall how tasty our food was. Conversation frequently drifted to talk about favorite drinks and favorite foods. It didn't help though. These thoughts made us feel terribly isolated. We prisoners hadn't realized at the time just how good our childhoods had been. Once we knew suffering, we could appreciate and agonize over the tormenting memories of food cast aside and only then we truly understood isolation and felt the pain of hunger.

I remember going with my father to the synagogue during holidays and sometimes on Shabbat. My mother used to go only on the major holidays. Otherwise, she was too busy preparing food. She used to make Galler[10], a tasty delicacy to me then and I love it to this day.

As kids, my friends and I used to enjoy watching the Polish army training close to the soccer fields. Though Jews served in the army, our observations were of the Poles. Watching the military march together and shouting, "yeden, dva, trzy!" or "one, two, three!" was a highlight of our free time.

One of my greatest childhood passions was soccer. Matches at the soccer field were a true highlight of my youth. We didn't have money to buy tickets so every Sunday a large group of kids would dig a hole under the wooden fence to sneak in and watch the game. These soccer games were one of our favorite forms of entertainment.

Sometimes I would go with my friends to a local pond on weekends. With our allowance money we would rent kayaks by the hour. I remember how dangerous it was because not one of us knew how to swim!

---

[10] A savory gelatin made from cows' leg bones; also called pacha.

Every summer, our family traveled to a special resort outside of Lodz to the east called Wiśniowa Góra[11]. We would travel there by train and then travel further in a traditional horse drawn carriage. Each year, for two months, we lived there carefree during June and July.

We would rent a cottage that had a central wood- and coal-burning stove. There was no electricity for lighting so we would use a petroleum lamp. The cottage consisted of one large shared room containing the beds and the kitchen; there was no indoor toilet, only an outhouse in the back. It was set in a very lush green in the middle of a forest full of pine trees. Oh, how we loved this summer resort!

During the week we would be with our mother. Our father would come up each weekend. We so looked forward to my father's arrival; we would wait impatiently at the station for his return. When he got out of the carriage, all three children would race to hug him

---

[11] A small village within Lodz East County.

screaming, "Tata, Tata!" I truly believe that seeing us when he arrived was one of his happiest life moments.

There was a pond nearby where our family would sometimes rent a rowboat. Often, we would go to the forest and pick blueberries. We would eat half and bring back the other half to share. Time at the river was spent attempting to catch fish and then throwing them back.

Everyone loved being in the country. My mother was happy to get away from the city. We had many friends there too, and we met people over the years.

Life in Poland was happy when I was young because my family had one another. In reflection, my parents struggled to provide for my family, however, as kids, we were oblivious to their hardships.

The Germans Invade Poland

September, 1939

My family knew a war was coming from the announcements on the radio. On September 1st, 1939, the Germans invaded Poland. We heard cannons firing outside of our building in Lodz. My father remembered the sounds of cannon fire from World War I and he had set up a good hiding spot from shots coming in from the west. We safely hid in a well-enforced stairwell of the building.

Within days of their occupation, the German army started implementing rules and laws against Jewish citizens. First, they forced all Jews to wear armbands with the Star of David. Then, the directions were changed to a yellow star to be worn on the outer left side of people's shirts with one also worn on the back. I believed those who did not comply were arrested or beaten. Some were released but later most were sent to concentration camps.

After a few weeks, over the course of two days in November 1939, the Germans set fire to all 14 of the synagogues in Lodz. Due to the German occupation there were terrible food shortages in Lodz. Jews were routinely pulled out of food lines; lines explicitly set up and formed for these shortages to ensure that everyone received bread and essentials. Jews removed from the line were often beaten; their crime was simply being Jewish.

By My Mother's Hand

The burning of the reform synagogue in Lodz, Poland on November 14, 1939

Once, while waiting in line for food with another hundred people, a German guard approached the crowd, came right up to me and said, "Disappear!" I am not sure why, but he made me run away. I do not know what happened to the rest of the crowd but I never saw any of those people again.

In February 1940, the Germans organized a ghetto for the Jews in the north part of Lodz. We Jews were forced to work menial jobs like carrying bricks, sweeping and other manual tasks. We were not paid for any of the labour and the work seemed endless.

Eventually, my brother Yosef couldn't take the oppression any more and smuggled himself out of Poland. He was only 19 years old and I considered him to be my best friend. I know that he made it to the other side of the Polish-Russian border. From the time of his departure until early 1941, I heard from Yosef through letters. It then became impossible to remain in touch. Yosef was in hiding in Kiev and then Harkov, cities that were in the Ukraine at the time. Eventually we lost touch altogether. To this day my only wish is to find out what happened to him. I have tried searching through the Red Cross and various organizations and agencies with no success.

In the middle of the night, during the winter near the beginning of February 1940, I heard footsteps along the staircase of our building. The Germans came into our apartment and forced us out. They took all our valuables and gave us less than ten minutes to gather what we could before transporting us to the police station.

All Jews were forced to surrender their radios. Radios were our main source for news and information about current events. From this point on, and for the duration of the war, my family and I were completely cut-off and unaware of what was happening in the outside world.

The Germans marched us to the police station and then to a settlement area (an empty factory building) mixed up with Polish people. They searched us for valuables and if they found any items of value they would shoot to kill. They then marched us to a railroad station into passenger cars with broken windows to be transported.

A few days later we arrived in occupied Southern Poland, in a town called Nowy Sącz, about twenty kilometers north of the Czechoslovakian border. There, we were unloaded and handed over to the local Jewish community.

This, I now understand, was all part of a plan to resettle 200,000 Jews and another 100,000 Poles out of Lodz to make room for German nationals from the Ukraine.

Arrival in Nowy Sącz

February, 1940

Nowy Sącz was a beautiful town surrounded by picturesque mountains, but its beauty completely escaped my notice. It was an especially bitter winter. In the painful cold we had to walk to the town from the railroad station and the Jewish community allowed us to sleep on the floor of the local synagogue. We truly thought that we would be resettled and the war wouldn't last long. Even in our worst nightmares we never imagined it would be five years. Before the resettlement of the Lodz Jews, Nowy Sącz's population was 35,000 of which 16,000 were Jews. My parents and I became part of the Jewish community of Nowy Sącz. The local Jews were very kind to us. They did all they could to help.

One time, shortly after our arrival, the Polish police, who worked under the Germans, caught me without my armband. In 1940, near the beginning of the war, I wasn't too fearful. However, I remember feeling uncertain as they took me to the police station. I didn't know what they would do to me; my greatest worry was that they could have sent me over to the Gestapo[12]. I quickly told them that I had changed my shirt and I forgot to switch the armband over. Fortunately, I was released unharmed. The majority of people in this area were Polish Jewish citizens who feared the Germans and almost all completely obeyed their rule.

I met a boy my age there named Nunek Eltzner and we became good friends. His parents tried to help us however they could. Generously, this family offered us pillows, sheets, cooking utensils, towels and packages of meat as his father was a butcher.

---

[12] An abbreviation of Geheime Staatspolizei; the Secret State Police of the Nazis.

An old photo of the great Synagogue in Nowy Sącz, built in 1746

Initially, my family lived out of the synagogue in Nowy Sącz. Eventually we were relocated by the Jewish administration to a very small one-room apartment in a nice building in the middle of town, on Jagiellońska Street.

The town was administrated by the German Gestapo. The Germans had enacted a law that forced Jews to work as slave labourers. It was clear we would be immediately put to work. The chief of the Gestapo in Nowy Sącz was Heinrich Hamann. I remember all the SS guards' names: Yohan, Lapitzski and Runov. They were my direct bosses and I witnessed them killing too many innocent people, young and old. My mother, my father and I were constantly upset and fearful. We never imagined such atrocities, never imagined that people could do such things. At 18 years old, I was afraid to even look at the Germans.

My first job was working in the Water Administration. I worked on regulating and redirecting rivers and streams that came down the Karpaty Mountains. Among many other Jews, I built concrete steps to redirect the water of one river to a bigger river. The water did not supply anyone with anything. This labour was created to generate backbreaking work and force innocent civilian Jews closer and closer to death.

My work required me to stand in water up to my knees every day from September to November regardless of weather conditions. The water was so painfully cold I often had frostbite on my toes. To relieve my feet, I would stand like a stork on one foot at a time. My feet were severely scraped from standing barefoot in water day after day. After November, the Germans could not force this particular form of labour further as the rivers froze over.

Next, I was assigned to assist the German army with relocating supplies. My task was to unload three carts of coal a day. By the end of each day my face was covered in coal dust and of course there were no proper shower facilities. The only positive part of my experience was that we were regularly fed. Not only did this mean that we ate beyond the portions of the starving, but also that I could collect food and trade it for other hard-to-get goods like a piece of butter or some coffee.

The manager of the army storage facility was Joseph Grime, a German from Sudetenland[13] and a veteran of World War I. He lost three fingers in that war. He was very kind to us, his slave labourers, by giving us extra food to take home to our families. He would give me a couple of loaves of bread per week, a great amount of sustenance at the time. Grime would buy the loaves from the army bakery for his people and always save some for his Jewish

---

[13] An area of Czechoslovakia.

slave labourers. This helped my parents as I had food to bring back to them.

One day, our group went out to work carrying our special passes to get to our jobs. Without passes, we would have been either shot or sent immediately to a concentration camp. This particular day, a Gestapo officer named Runov stopped us. He checked our passes and wanted to take us to the office of the Gestapo. We told Runov that we had our passes; we showed them to him, but for whatever reason, he wanted us to go to the Gestapo office. Instead, we persuaded him to come back with us to discuss his concerns with Grime as we were not too far from the army storage facility and Grime was compassionate towards us.

When we arrived at our workplace, Grime saw us with Runov. He took the officer inside his office and told us, "Don't worry, I will fix this if there is a problem." Grime was very friendly with the Gestapo and a very influential man. Grime made sure nothing happened to us.

At one point, there were many arrests in the Jewish area of town. Grime had knowledge of these events and would not allow us to return home after work. Without the soldiers' permission or knowledge, Grime arranged for us to stay in an old building not far from the storage facility, in an empty ammunitions dump for the Polish army. There were sleeping quarters with bunk beds and an oven for cooking food. He also made sure wood shavings were spread on the floor because there was no solidly constructed floor. I remember I was terrified that the whole building could go up in flames because of those wood shavings. The Nazis arrested many people that night and sent them to the Rožnov and Lipie labour camps where people performed slave labour to construct a river dam.

Grime occasionally sent me to work at the headquarters of the military administration on Jagiellońska Street; a three story building belonging to Dr. Amaizen, a local Jew. There, I was responsible for looking after the garden; watering the plants inside the building, sweeping, painting, and general maintenance. Grime's wife was responsible for the kitchen where they prepared food for the military unit administrators. When lunchtime came around she never forgot me. Calling me to the rear entrance through the courtyard she would give me any leftover food.

Once, Grime sent me with a few boys on a large truck with several German soldiers through the outlying areas to the east of town. We were charged with dismantling the bunks where the German soldiers slept on their way to the Russian front. The wooden bunk beds were arranged in the barns of Polish farms. We took them apart, loaded them onto trucks and would return them to the army storage facility.

On one farm the German soldiers found some firewood hidden away that the local farmer took from the Germans. They captured the farmer and loaded him on the truck to be punished later. On another farm, they confiscated a pig. It was my job to pull the pig by its ears and walk it through the local marketplace to the slaughterhouse. I remember thinking that the pig knew where it was going because it was squealing the whole way. This was the first time I had ever encountered a pig, never mind pull it by its ears. The slaughterer hit the pig between the eyes with an axe and then started cutting the corpse to pieces.

We made our way back to headquarters with the soon-to-be punished farmer. En route, we passed a wooded area and the driver stopped the truck. They ordered the farmer to get off the truck and had him stand next to a tree. One soldier took out his gun and seemed about to shoot the farmer. In my mind, I knew they would not shoot him since I had worked with these particular soldiers, and they were kind to me. I was correct; they were just scaring and intimidating the poor farmer. After they noticed his knees shaking, a soldier shouted, "So you want to run away now? Go ahead, run, run!" They let the farmer run away once their need for amusement was fulfilled. The rest of us were brought back to town.

By this time, my parents and I had spent nearly two and a half years in Nowy Sącz.

The Ghetto in Nowy Sącz

May, 1941

While we were away from our home town, the Germans had created the Lodz Ghetto, closed to the public by April 1940. All Jews that lived across the city were supposed to be transferred to the ghetto. They were catching Jews in the streets and arresting them.

On June 22, 1941, at the German-Russian border, the Germans attacked the Soviet Union and the German army then moved east rapidly. German troops and battalions would come through and station for a day in Nowy Sącz and then continue eastwards. Grime, our boss, used to come in when we had lunch and always said, "Oh, Stalin and the Führer[14] are one hand," meaning, Stalin and Hitler are good friends. The day the Germans attacked he said, "Stalin is a pig! He double-crossed the Führer!"

At that time, the Nazis created a ghetto in Nowy Sącz. My parents and I had to move to that ghetto during May 1941. I had a pass to leave the ghetto only to go to work. Whenever there was trouble in the ghetto, Grime would not let our group go back home after work to keep us safe.

One day, going out to work, all were diverted to the Gestapo office where Heinriech Hamann was the chief. They had some sort of a list; whoever appeared on that list was arrested. I waited anxiously through the reciting of names. My name was not called. I did not know it then, but all Jews on that list were members of a Jewish socialist organization. Afterwards, the SS came into the ghetto and started arresting people. They collected all of the arrested, approximately three hundred Jews in total.

---

[14] German title meaning leader or guide, referring to Adolf Hitler.

From there they were marched to the Jewish cemetery where there was a huge pre-dug grave. They were all massacred by gunfire. Everyone could hear the shooting. We were all fearful and we couldn't intervene. We had no power, no control.

Heinriech Hamann, Chief of the Gestapo in Nowy Sącz

My parents and I were fortunate to live in the first building near the ghetto entrance in a small room on the third floor. Our door looked like a small entrance to an attic so it was somewhat concealed. The night after the massacre, twenty Gestapo officers came into the ghetto and entered many buildings, including ours. All those they approached they shot without question. I stood frozen in shock, staring out of our window above and watched the Gestapo officers arbitrarily killing people in the courtyard. They broke windows and doors and shot children and the elderly, everyone they approached. Our staircase was dark; perhaps because of this they did not venture up to find our small room. I felt myself shaking; we were all terrified. We felt helpless and my father tried to calm us. All we heard all night was shooting and screaming.

After what seemed like a half-hour, a woman came running into our room. She had two holes in her throat, bleeding out of both sides from a bullet wound. My father grabbed a towel and pressed it over her neck. She stayed with us overnight. Her twelve-year-old daughter and two sons, aged six and four, were all shot in the head at close range by the Gestapo. Her daughter died on the spot but the boys survived a few weeks and then died. This poor mother, she survived the ordeal.

At least one hundred Jews were massacred that day. We later found out that Hamann ordered the killings to take place because he had a personal dispute with his deputy, a man named Miller. Hamann really wanted to kill Miller so he attempted to set up a situation so he could explain Millers death by accusing the Jews as being responsible for shooting his deputy. Miller was indeed shot but he survived with injuries and was able to describe Hamann's attempt at murdering a fellow officer. After his recovery, Miller was relocated.

The next morning, once it was quiet, leaders of the Jewish community gave orders to bury the dead and take the wounded to the hospital. At the time, the leader of the Jewish community was Yankel Marin. He travelled to Krakow to the governors' office and tried to get Hamann replaced by a different SS officer. However, Yankel did not realize what Hamann was capable of. Hamann heard of Yankel's plan, arrested him and sent him to Auschwitz.

Within three weeks, an urn with the ashes of Yankel Marin arrived in the ghetto. I remember listening silently as my father told us this story.

Eventually, I lost my favourable job working under Grime because the storage facility was moved to a location closer to the German army. I was assigned a new job working with the German air force with another five boys from the ghetto. We would leave the ghetto in the morning and return at night. We did whatever we were told; sweeping, gardening, painting, cleaning, anything they told us to do.

One day on my way home to the ghetto, I noticed announcements posted on the ghetto buildings: "For strategic reasons, Jews can no longer remain here. They will be sent to the east to be concentrated in camps to work." The Jews in the ghetto truly believed, as it happened in the past, that they would be sent elsewhere to work. I remember saying to my parents, "we have been resettled once already from our homes and we will be resettled again. What can they do to me? I am not afraid of doing work!"

The date of the announcement was August 1942. This was a half-year after the Wannsee Conference[15] took place. At this conference the German leaders came together and announced the "Final Solution"; the plan to completely exterminate the Jewish population from Europe.

---

[15] The Wannsee Conference took place in Wannsee, a wealthy suburb of Berlin, on January 20th, 1942, the conference detailing the "Final Solution of the Jewish Question."

The Nowy Sącz Ghetto Liquidation

August, 1942

A few days before the scheduled ghetto resettlement day, I was working at the air force base. A high-ranking German officer approached me and said, "I heard about the resettling but I would like you boys to stay in town and work for me." I told him my name, not daring to ask his, and he ordered me to call the other boys to get their names. He wrote our names on a piece of paper and he said he would ask for us during the ghetto resettlement assembly.

On the day we assembled to begin our "resettlement," the entire Jewish population of the ghetto was present. Approximately 16,000 innocent Jews stood on the riverbank between two bridges facing the opposite town. I watched as the high-ranking officer, who three days earlier had asked for my name and the names of my friends, gave Heinrich Hamann the short list of names. My mother had told me before that if I could remain in the town instead of going along with the resettlement it was more likely that I would survive. However, I had made up my mind earlier that I would, no matter what, stay with my parents.

I was first on the list and Hamann called out my name. I wanted to stay with my parents so I did not respond. As he called my name for the second time, my mother forcefully pushed me out of the lineup. By my mother's hand, I stumbled a few meters ahead of the group. The soldiers pulled me aside and then the rest of the boys were summoned.

Once we were retrieved, Hamann called on the community leaders and the Jewish police, approximately two hundred people, and they took us all away to return to a special area within the ghetto. That shove my mother gave me saved my life, but it was also the last time I would ever see my parents. That was when my childhood ended. From then onwards, I was on my own.

The remaining people, including my parents, were sent back to a small part of the ghetto. For several nights they were crammed into a tiny living area. They were forced to sleep on staircases because it was so crowded where they stayed.

Over the next three days, my parents and the group of Jews from the Nowy Sącz ghetto were liquidated, loaded onto trains and transported directly to Bełżec. Bełżec, a death camp in Poland on the Ukrainian border, was created as part of the "Final Solution."[16] The entire group, including my mother and father, were murdered upon their arrival. After the war, I learned that approximately 600,000 Jews were murdered at Bełżec

---

[16] The Final Solution was Hitler's plan to systematically carry out the genocide of European Jews during World War II.

during the camp's one year of operation until the end of 1942.

If not for the German officer who wrote down my name, I would not be here to share my story. I never saw him again. I do not know why he decided to take down the names of us six young Jewish boys. I like to believe he knew what was going to happen and wanted to save the few he could. Though I never knew his name, I do know that he saved our lives.

After a few days, while the Nowy Sącz Ghetto was being emptied out, the Nazis did not let us go back to the air force base to work. They charged the team of two hundred remaining to clean up the ghetto. Our orders were to remove the belongings and furniture from all the houses and apartments. It was a hard job as everything was made from heavy oak, not like today's furniture, which is often made of cheap particleboard. We did our jobs although we were very weak because we were not given rations that were even remotely adequate.

We had to unload everything we had found onto the streets and then onto trucks going to an unknown destination. The ghetto had become a ghost town. There were so few people and no other sound but the scattering of feathers, papers and fragmented glass as they flew about in the wind.

Eventually, I found myself cleaning out the apartment where I lived with my parents. It was a very painful and isolating experience, especially to see the walls and bed where my parent used to sleep less than a week ago. Although I felt sad, I had truly believed that the war would end and we would be together again.

Often, our small group would go to the edge of the fence of the ghetto courtyard to meet Christian Poles. We would sell some of the items we had emptied from the buildings through the fence in exchange for food. We were fortunate that we were only 200 people; because of this the Germans didn't watch the back of the fences. We sold whatever we could find – pillows, blankets or clothing – and the Poles gave us food in exchange.

There were a few Jews left who worked in groups outside the ghetto. One of my friends, Nunek Elsner, a Jewish policeman, was the leader of one of these groups.

One time he arrived at the ghetto after curfew and the Gestapo threatened to kill him as punishment. Nunek told the officers his parents had buried valuables in their backyard and if they would spare him, he could lead them to the valuables. He took them to the spot and dug up the items. The valuables were buried in the backyard by Nunek's parents out of fear they would not survive. He gave all the valuables to the soldiers. The officers took him to Chełmiec, a suburb outside of Nowy Sącz, where they shot him dead.

In November 1942, we finished cleaning out the ghetto. One evening after work we were suddenly surrounded by armed Polish police, lined up in rows and marched to the city jail. We were searched for valuables and stripped of all our belongings. I managed to hide a little bit of money for myself in a small pocket I had behind my belt. I was lucky it was not found or I would surely have been killed.

The next morning, we were assembled in the jail courtyard where we stood in front of ten to fifteen Gestapo officers. I recognized almost all of them;

Hamann, Lapitsky, Runov and Yohan were there. They were standing with long leather coats and machine guns draped over their shoulders. Whenever they wore leather coats we knew it was a sign they were going to kill people. The coats prevented blood from splattering on their clothing. They arranged us into rows of five. It was late November, and the first snow had just started. We stood paralyzed and in complete silence, trembling and terrified they would direct us to the cemetery which meant we would be killed. However, instead, they ordered us to march to the railroad station where we were loaded into train cars with SS guards. After several hours we arrived in a bigger town called Tarnów.

The Tarnów Ghetto

November, 1942

Tarnów was a small city about seventy kilometers northeast of Nowy Sącz. Before the war, its population was 56,000; 25,000 of which were Jews. Once the Germans invaded, a ghetto was established for the Jews of Tarnów. After Jews from surrounding villages were forced to move into the ghetto, the Jewish population exceeded 40,000. However, by the time we arrived, there were only about 4,000 Jews remaining. The rest were sent to Bełżec death camp.

I was put in a section of the ghetto called Ghetto A, which was reserved for Jews who did not have work. I lived in a basement with fifteen other young boys.

We were permitted to go once a day to the kitchen for our daily dose of watery soup. This was not nearly enough, so we had to find other ways to sustain ourselves.

I had a friend who was a baker, and he would bake buns in the ghetto bakery. Together we would climb over the fence with the buns to Ghetto B, where we would sell them to Jews coming back from work. I would buy flour with the złoty[17] we made and bake more buns. I did this a few times until my money ran out. We were so hungry, but every time we would eat a bun, we were literally eating our profits. Slowly we were left with no more buns, no flour, and no money.

The ghetto residents that were sent to the concentration camps did not have any time to even pack personal belongings or take bedding, clothes and essentials along with them. Some left sheets and

---

[17] Polish currency

pillowcases to air out. Early in the evenings, we used to walk around the ghetto looking for left-over bedding or pillows to take. On the upper levels of the buildings we would nudge any bedding we found over the edge of the balcony so it would fall to the ground below so we could collect it. Taking their possessions never felt like stealing; we were taking it from our own people in order to survive.

We found an empty room in the basement of our building. There, I would cut the bedding material and let out the feathers. Then I would hide the remaining cloth under my shirt. When the SS officers on guard duty would go around the corner from us, I raced to a hole we found in the ghetto fence. Earlier, we hid the hole by covering it with a wooden board. I quickly removed the board and flew through the hole in the fence. On the other side of the street was what we felt was the "real world."

Terrified, I had to run like a cat across the street while I concealed the white and blue star on my armband. I would approach any Polish Christian family home that I saw. I would knock on their doors and the occupants would shudder from shock when they saw how emaciated I looked from not eating. We would do business by exchanging the bedding gathered from the ghetto for small amounts of bread. The Poles had little, but my friends and I did not have any food whatsoever. I did this many times. Looking back, I shake when I think about the huge risks I took. Had I been caught, I surely would have been shot on the spot.

I had a girlfriend in the ghetto; we shared the same courtyard. Her name was Chana. She was a nice girl, shorter than me, with long flowing dark hair. She appeared one day in our room in the basement just to talk. A local from Tarnów, she was two or three years younger than me (I was nineteen at the time). When I would sneak out beyond the Ghetto walls for food, I would bring back some bread for Chana and her mother. She had a sister and brother sent to live in Ghetto B, where they were put to work. Chana used to make me laugh and together we would forget where we were, at least for a moment. Her family helped me as well, mostly by sharing the soup her mother made.

Nobody in Ghetto A worked, including Chana. We would walk in the evening together, holding hands. She was my first love and also my first kiss, right there in our courtyard. We used to talk about how we would see our families again when the war ended. She dreamed of becoming a teacher after the war. Chana and I promised each other that if we both survived, we would marry.

Once, on the way to the ghetto kitchen, Chana and I saw a group of SS officers. Suddenly, everyone was running away. Grunov, the most feared Gestapo officer in Tarnów, was approaching with a carriage carrying two Jews – a man and a woman. It was obvious he was going to shoot them. Grunov instructed them to get out of the carriage. I stood paralyzed in a staircase by a window looking into the courtyard, watching the whole time. I observed Grunov's arm raise and point at their heads with his pistol. He shot twice and blew a hole through the back of each of their heads. They fell right away, face down to the ground. All I could think was "murderers!" I had just witnessed murder and I was powerless to do anything. I could not imagine why Grunov had shot them. Maybe they were caught as Jews outside the ghetto.

After shooting them and terrifying all the observers, he probably went and spoke with the Jewish authorities about the crimes for which Grunov believed they were responsible.

Around the same time, there were rumors spreading in the ghetto that the Germans were looking for young girls and boys to send to a new concentration camp, but we did not know why or for what. Nobody wanted to go to a camp where the SS surround you with towers and walls. All we knew was that no one ever came back from those camps.

Because of these rumors, my friend Moishe Leizer Bergman and I decided to hide in a shed in the courtyard to avoid being chosen. This was during early spring and it was cold after the sun set. We would sit there overnight, frozen. There was no heating in our room in the basement, but at least it was warmer than outside. In the morning, no one came looking for us, so we decided to return to the basement.

A few minutes after we arrived at our basement a Jewish police officer entered and grabbed us. Chana watched as the police officer led us out of the basement and she followed us onto the street. I was devastated to be leaving her and to have been caught. I didn't know why or where they were going to take me. All I thought about were the rumors that they needed labourers for a new camp. I was still confident there was a real need for labourers. I had no way of knowing that that would be the last time I ever saw Chana.

The Jewish police turned us over to the SS who then took us to a police station and kept us overnight in the basement without food or water. When they counted one hundred boys and girls, we were loaded onto trucks with guards and taken east of Tarnów, to a camp called Szebnie, about 70 kilometers to the southeast.

After the war, while traveling from town to town on a coal train with my friends, I happened to recognize Chana's sister. She told me that upon their arrival Chana and her mother were immediately selected for the gas chambers at Auschwitz.

At Szebnie Camp

April, 1943

Moshe and I traveled to Szebnie on open trucks with SS guards watching over us with handguns and Czech rifles. Szebnie was different than the ghettos I stayed in up to this point. It was a concentration camp with twelve-foot-high barbed wire fences and SS men sitting within tall towers. Almost immediately after getting off the truck, I was whipped over the head by an SS officer. My crime was not removing my school cap in his presence.

The one-yard-long whips the SS enjoyed using were made from the skeletons of umbrellas. Four or five of the dense wires were connected together, covered with leather and attached to a handle. I saw stars in the daylight sky after each whipping.

We were brought inside to a room where we were searched again for valuables. If the officers found anything, they would shoot. The whole local SS administration was on hand. The SS officers lived outside the camp in nicer barracks and slept in comfortable beds, whereas we slept in wooden bunks without mattresses. We slept on wood shavings.

At Szebnie, like all the concentration camps I would enter, there was roll call. This always occurred in the Appelplatz[18], a large area in the center of the camp. There were already approximately two hundred people present from Kraków-Płaszów concentration camp (the camp filmed in Schindler's List). In total, we were about three

---

[18] Roll call square, usually the center of the concentration camp, where the Nazis would make their victims stand as they were counted and identified as numbers. There they were frequently made to witness hangings, executions, and further selections.

hundred prisoners. Over our stay in Szebnie, other prisoners were brought from surrounding cities and towns. Eventually Szebnie held a few thousand innocent Jewish prisoners.

Roll call was always done by Komendant Scheid, or as we would call him "shed," which means devil in Hebrew. During the first roll call I witnessed, Scheid said, "Today is payday… someone will get an award for misbehaving." They called out a random Jewish man. Scheid gave one of his SS men an order to whip him twenty five times. This chosen man had to lie over a specially-made stool. When the whipping started so did the man's screaming. Scheid did not like that, so he gave another SS man the order to shoot. The second SS man took out his gun, told the Jew to turn around, and shot him in the head. The man fell down and two boys, that I would later learn were the Turner brothers, took him from camp in their two-wheeled buggy so they could bury him. Beside me stood a fourteen-year-old boy. It was his father that was just killed in front of us all. He stood there bearing witness to this event. He could not move, could not cry. He was just frozen there. I don't know what happened to the boy, but he must have been in so much pain to witness his father's death this way. This was our warm welcome to Szebnie.

One Sunday afternoon, Scheid came into the camp and called for our Jewish Komendant[19] and asked him why his labourers were not working. The Jew explained that Sunday afternoon was our break time to take showers, to get haircuts and rest. At that moment a young red-headed boy ran by. Scheid suddenly stopped him. He said to the boy, "Oh, are you running away because you don't want to shower?" He then took out his gun and shot the young boy in the back of the head. His twin sister witnessed the whole ordeal. I stood maybe six feet behind Scheid and she was about five feet away from me. She knew she could not react. What could she do? If she reacted, Scheid would surely shoot her too.

After the shooting, Scheid, known so well for his cruelty, said to our Jewish Komendant that he could shower the whole camp in half an hour. He gave an order

---

[19] A Jew appointed to represent the whole camp.

to bring fifty boys and fifty girls and to have them undress outside. I was among those chosen. The whole SS administration enjoyed a Sunday afternoon show. After undressing, the girls tried to hide their bodies, as did the men, including me. Scheid said that if any of the boys would have an erection, they would be shot. We were then forced into a shower room with the SS watching and laughing. The officers let out a little bit of cold water to sprinkle on our heads. Then, the next group was called until the entire camp was showered in this way. The SS officers were very sadistic and humiliated us at every opportunity.

A different time, the Hauptscharführer [20] Grzymek, a German national who understood Polish, came in with his four police guards. The guards were weaponless Jews from the Ordnungsdienst[21]. Grzymek carried a machine gun over his shoulder. I know now that it was a Russian Kalashnikov rifle. He wanted to test out his weapon. Nearby, there were boys digging a hole in the ground.

---

[20] Leader of the camp.

[21] Unarmed Jewsh police mobilized by the Nazis to control prisoners of the camp.

This was a meaningless daily job they were ordered to do. Grzymek called one of these boys over to him and asked the boy to bend over. The boy did not want to obey so Grzymek grabbed his head and forcefully pushed him down. The boy somehow managed to move away a few feet. Grzymek could not believe that a Jewish boy would not obey and did not want to be killed. He commanded the Jewish police to grab this poor boy and hang him in the roll call square on a pole with his arms tied elevated behind his back.

The boy screamed throughout the day from pain. As his arms were slowly pulled out of their sockets, his feet started to touch the ground. When this happened the hole under the boy was dug a little deeper. He begged for someone to kill him, to put him out of his misery.

At that time I was working in a mechanical laundry facility, cleaning the clothes of death camp victims. I had made a knife from metal scraps I found in the facility. I kept it hidden to use for dividing bread amongst my friends (if we tore the bread, it would not be divided evenly). I could have used this knife to end the boy's suffering, but I was too afraid to help him. I did not want to take a risk partly because I wanted to live, but also because the entire camp lived in fear of the repercussions that would be imposed on the entire camp if anyone intervened.

The boy hung there until the nighttime roll call. We all stood around the hanging boy. By this time we were a few thousand people standing together at the camp's roll call square.

The SS administration arrived in their vehicles. One of the administrators stood up inside his car so that he would be visible to everyone. He pointed to the hanging boy and said, "This boy put all your lives in danger today. He attacked the Lagerfuhrer[22] Grzymek. Because of this boy we might have killed all of you today. But, by the order of the Komendant, nobody will be harmed today except for the hanging boy." He then gave the order to take the boy down.

---

[22] Commander of the camp.

With the boy lying face down on the ground, arms still tied behind his back, Grzymek finally got to use his Kalashnikov. He shot a few bullets straight into the boy's head. Blood splashed on the soil. The whole square seemed red from his blood. The Turner brothers were ready again with their buggy.

The Turner brother's buggy had a hidden compartment in the bottom. While being sent to bury dead bodies, they would exchange valuables for food with Ukrainian SS guards who could be bribed. The Ukrainian SS men would deal with Polish farmers for us. They would give the farmers goods we found on dead people like clothes, gold teeth or other valuables people had hidden. These goods were exchanged for any food offered by the farmers. The brothers stored the food they got from the guards in the hidden compartment in the buggy.

During the next roll call, the Nazis brought in ten Jewish men and women. There were rumors that these Jews were planning an escape. They were tied up with their arms behind their backs. They were pushed face-down to the ground. The Komendant shouted, "Whoever looks away or blinks an eye will be put here next on the ground." Then, the SS shot with their Kalashnikovs back and forth across the line of men and women. If a body was still moving they would finish the job with their handguns. Three thousand people watched this terrible event sickened and horrified. Nobody knew who would be next.

Many times at roll call, the Nazis randomly chose five hundred people. Nobody knew what they were being punished for or what they had done. The people were brought outside the camp next to a ravine. They had to undress and then they were all shot and killed. A truck loaded with twelve young male prisoners left the camp and never returned. These prisoners were ordered to burn the dead bodies by the ravine. The Nazis were careful not to have any witnesses. I could hear the shooting and then I would see and smell the black smoke at night as the ravine was just a half-mile outside of the camp. Everyone knew it was a lost cause; we were all stuck in a cage and treated like animals. Many times, I thought I would be next.

Living in Szebnie was constant terror. However, over time, I somehow became accustomed to it. I started to feel hardened despite the horrors I witnessed.

Szebnie Liquidation

November, 1943

At the start of November, 1943, there were rumors that the camp was to be decommissioned. There were about 4,500 people left living within the camp. Einsatzgruppen [23] arrived in the hundreds with machine guns and other weaponry. I knew they were going to liquidate but I didn't know if they were going to take us out to the ravine and kill us all or take us to another camp. The next morning they entered the camp; some went up

---

[23] A special squad of the SS.

on the roofs of our buildings to point their machine guns at us. They chose five hundred men to remain behind in Szebnie but I was not chosen to be part of this group. I could have been chosen because I was one of the first that arrived at Szebnie and I had established connections that would have allowed me to stay behind. This time, however, I decided I would go wherever I was told. I had a feeling that this time I should just follow the majority.

Lagerführer Grzymek stood up on a stool and said, "Who said we were going to kill you? That's not true. We are going to send you to a new camp where each and every one of you will have a bed. Here you have nothing – you are sleeping on wood shavings. Don't forget to take blankets with you for the children (there were five remaining) so they won't be cold."

When it got dark outside the SS marched us out in groups of fifty. They created a corridor between vehicles parked in a row with their lights on along the road, and every few meters stood an armed guard. We marched quietly for a few kilometers to a small railroad station called Moderówka. When we arrived at the loading ramp of the station a train was waiting. We realized quickly that it was not a passenger train but a closed cattle train. Each car had a little window obstructed with barbed wire.

The SS started beating us. They hit us with the butt ends of their rifles and screamed for us to undress. I threw off my coat and tied my shoes together.

I was one of the last to board the packed full cattle car. There was a bucket for excrement that filled fast and was over-running. Looking behind me I saw huge piles of clothing on the ramp. During this whole ordeal, the guards were drinking. By the time we had removed our clothes the officers were drunk and did not know what they were doing. They shoved us all in, tightly squished together. I was standing up beside the little window, and they closed the door. The train traveled west. Some prisoners who started their journey from the west of Poland said that only one camp exists in the direction we were going – a camp by the name of Auschwitz. I knew that Auschwitz was a camp that one could not survive for long.

Apparently, of the five hundred men left behind in Szebnie, only seventy were left alive. Four hundred and thirty were immediately killed in the ravine. The Nazis did not want more than seventy people left alive. Most likely, I would have been among those killed. In retrospect, I made the right decision to stay with the majority. I only found out about this final act of horror after the war, after meeting one of the seventy remaining survivors of Szebnie. I know at least one man of the seventy survived the Holocaust; I met him after the war in 1949 or 1950 in Tel Aviv. His last name was Elsner. He was the deputy chief of the Jewish Police and a kind man.

The Road to Auschwitz

November, 1943

I was standing beside one of the blocked up cattle car windows when the train stopped at a station en route. My friend Moshe Leizer Bergman was standing beside me. I was talking to him when suddenly I heard somebody scream at me, "Quiet!" Then, I heard a very loud blast and did not know what was going on. I saw stars in front of my eyes and heard ringing in my ears as I fell down. I grabbed my head and gratefully, I realized I was still alive. I stood up and felt my head again and noticed that my hair was singed. Soldiers at the station had shot at me because I was talking with Moshe. They missed my head by a quarter of an inch. I could smell my hair burning. I didn't know what to think; I just knew that I was so close to death. If the bullet flew an inch lower, it would have gone through my brain.

A few more days passed. I believe we were on the train for three or four days. Truthfully, I lost count. We had absolutely nothing to eat or drink the entire journey. Finally, we arrived at Auschwitz on the Judenrampe[24].

We arrived as a group of 4,500 prisoners; men, women and children, most but not all from our original group from Szebnie. The doors of the train opened and we were forced quickly out of the cars. I could see people wearing clothes that I had never seen before – uniforms that looked like unusual striped pajamas. These "funny-looking" Jewish prisoners helped to organize us. I believe this was done intentionally so that we would not be alarmed; they spoke to us in Yiddish and Polish. The prisoners told us that "going to the left side is no good,"

---

[24] The railroad station at Auschwitz where Jews were unloaded; direct translation means the "Jew Ramp."

and instructed us to say that we are technical workers - engineers, mechanics or electricians.

First, the women and their children were separated from the men and then we were formed into rows of five. We walked forward in formation as an SS officer screened each of us. As I approached the front, I heard an officer ask people about their age and profession. I noticed that if they said a shoemaker, tailor, or bookkeeper, they went to the left. When someone mentioned they were a carpenter or mechanic, they went to the right.

When my turn came, I did not wait until asked. I jumped straight ahead like a soldier the way I believed the Nazis preferred and told the officer I was an electro-mechanic and was twenty-one years old, though I was really only twenty. With his finger, he pointed to the right. In reality, I knew nothing about electro mechanics. I did not even finish high school but at least temporarily, I knew I had saved my own life.

My friend Moshe Bergman stood beside me but was sent to the left. That was the last time I ever saw Moshe. I realized later that it was because he was wearing glasses.

Of course, at the time, we did not know that people with glasses were deemed "undesirable" by the Nazis.

Almost fifty years later, while visiting Poland on the March of the Living program, I saw a room full of glasses collected from the prisoners sent to their deaths at Auschwitz. I thought about Moshe, and felt certain his glasses must be hidden somewhere within this pile. Since nobody suggested he remove his glasses before the selection, his glasses were all that remained.

Approximately three hundred women and nine hundred men, myself included, were selected. All the rest, more than three thousand people, would never be seen again. They were sent to the gas chambers, murdered for being Jews.

Our remaining group was chased by SS men with vicious dogs like German Shepherds, Rottweilers and Dobermans; dogs specially trained to attack people. I was forced to run on gravel paths with bare feet. My feet quickly began bleeding. I ran like this all the way to

Birkenau, a camp that was another part of Auschwitz approximately three kilometers away[25].

As we approached, I could see the lights on the fences of Birkenau and the guard towers a few feet away from the fences. The guard towers were not inside the camp, but outside. I noticed this from the distance but there was no time to think as we were forced to run. Those who could not run fast enough to keep up were at the mercy of the dogs. I understood very quickly that it was not good to remain near the end of any group.

---

[25] Auschwitz was a group of several concentration and death camps. It was made up of Auschwitz I (the Stammlager or main camp), Auschwitz II - Birkenau (the Vernichtungslager or extermination camp), Auschwitz III - Buna-Monowitz (a labour camp) as well as forty five other camps in the area.

Life in Auschwitz II - Birkenau

November, 1943

We arrived at Birkenau and we were immediately brought into a large barrack with hardly any room even to stand. We were told to sit on the floor and we could hear the structure creaking from our weight. By this time there were no more women or children with us. Only men had survived this last selection.

First, we met the Blokalteste[26]. Our block leader was a Jewish criminal sent from jail to Auschwitz. Before the

---

[26] The leader of a block of barracks.

war, our Blokalteste was arrested for making soap and illegally passing it off as a brand name not his own. He was sentenced to serve jail time. The Germans sent all Jewish and non-Jewish criminals to Auschwitz. He wore the symbol that criminals wore – a green triangle with a yellow triangle above it to form the Star of David.

The Star of David I wore was made up of a red triangle pointing down and on top of it, a yellow triangle pointing up. The red triangle was designated for political prisoners. All Jews wore a yellow and red star, except for those that were criminals. A black triangle pointing down was for Gypsies, purple for clergy, and pink for homosexuals.

Sitting in the barrack and seeing a fellow Jew, the prisoners started asking the Blokalteste where the washroom is or where they can get a drink of water. He replied, "You don't know where you are? Look, my parents went to the gas chambers and you want a drink of water and a toilet?"

After a little while in the barracks, we were ordered to take off the rest of our clothing – underwear, pants, whatever we still had on. We were then chased to another barrack where we had to register. There were tables lined up with SS men ready to record our names and place and date of birth. We had our arms tattooed with our assigned prisoner numbers. With the writing down of our names, they were literally removed from our identity. I then became prisoner 160993.

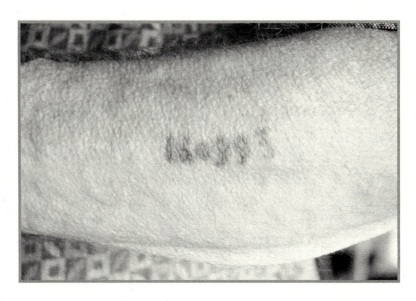

Henry's tattoo from Auschwitz as it appears at time of writing; prisoner number 160993

They cut off all our hair and we were brought into the shower room to have some water sprinkled on our heads. Then we went through the disinfecting process. We passed through a tunnel while getting patted on the head with rags by existing prisoners. This was their job at the camp. We then received our striped shirt and pants. The cloth felt so rough; I read later that the clothes were actually made of wood, though it was apparent as there were often some large pieces of wood in the cloth. They used prisoners to cut the wood, they used prisoners to shovel coal, and they used prisoners to create the uniforms.

Birkenau was a horrible place. There were four chimneys in view. At first I did not know how the chimneys were used. Existing prisoners explained that the chimneys were part of the crematoriums for the gas chambers. I saw smoke coming out during the day and flames during the night. It never stopped. The constant smell of burning flesh in the air was indescribable, beyond horrible.

I had heard about Auschwitz before but I did not know it was a death factory. I figured out that it was going to be impossible to survive in Auschwitz for more than a very short length of time. The surviving men from my camp stayed in a barrack called "quarantine camp," beside the Gypsy camp. Prisoners always tried to run away from Auschwitz; many were hunted down and killed trying to escape.

After six weeks of being at the quarantine camp, the Germans went through a further selection process. They were looking for those that had an electrical or construction background – carpenters, electricians, or bricklayers. Again, everyone had to undress completely and stand in rows. The SS men wrote down the numbers of the people they wanted. I was among those selected.

Later, we were called by number, loaded onto trucks and brought to Auschwitz I. There, we were undressed again, showered, and changed clothing. We had to stitch our numbers, made of linen, to the top left pocket of our shirt and also on the side of our pants. Then, we were re-loaded onto trucks and driven away to Auschwitz III,

Buna-Monowitz. It was only five to six kilometers away from Birkenau, but at least we would no longer be forced to bear the pain and the horror of the scent of constantly burning Jewish-human flesh. I was relieved to leave, wherever it meant I would be going.

Auschwitz III (Buna-Monowitz)

December, 1943

After arriving at Buna-Monowitz we were assigned to build a factory for a company called I.G. Farben, a subsidiary of Bayer[27]. They hoped to manufacture synthetic fuel and rubber. 10,000 prisoners were at hand, the majority being Jews. The factory's name was the Buna Werke.

---

[27] Bayer AG is a chemical and pharmaceutical company founded in Barmen, Germany in 1863.

I was assigned to a working squad designated to roll out huge concrete pipes. My job was to carry two cement bags one on top of the other on my back, all day long. We were given shoes. The soles of our shoes were made of wood and the upper part was made of leather.

Once while working, I did not notice that my foot was directly under a large concrete pipe and it rolled over my toes. Being winter, my foot was cold and numb but my big toe got squashed and actually cracked like a nut. I could not do anything about it and continued to work. Eventually it healed and the nail fell off. I was already so weak, I realized that I would not last very long if I continued this type of work.

One day as I was carrying cement bags, I noticed a German soldier out on the road outside the perimeter fence. He was transporting potatoes with a horse and buggy. I called him "Herr Unter Offizier," knowingly calling out a rank higher than he was to flatter him. I asked him to please throw me some potatoes through the fence, and surprisingly, he did. I hid them in my shirt and brought them with me.

I still had a problem - how could I eat raw potatoes? I noticed that at the end of our barrack there was a long radiator under the windows. I also noticed that on the outside of the barrack, there was a pipe letting out a powerful jet of steam. I took a metal can, made a few holes in the bottom, attached a handle with a piece of wire, and hung the can over the steam outlet. The steam cooked the potatoes as I watched from afar. I was constantly afraid someone would catch me so I did not wait very long before retrieving the can. The potatoes were not completely cooked, but they were edible. I quickly ate a few.

The camp was run by German prisoners. That they were criminals was clear because they wore the green triangles of criminal prisoners. I decided to take a risk and I walked into the administration building and asked them to change my job. Usually they threw prisoners out for asking such questions. I told them I came as an electro-mechanic and I was working on concrete pipes. I explained I would be much more useful as an electro-mechanic. They tested me with a few questions about electricity; about alternating and direct current. Using what I remembered from school, I answered. I spoke rapidly, flooding them with information about Ohm's law[28] and its formula. The next thing I knew, I was given a paper with permission to transfer to an electricians' squad.

I got moved to a new barrack where the electricians lived. My new Blokalteste's last name was Rand. He was a German Jew and thankfully, he was very good to me. If someone needed holes drilled or something sawed, being an "electrician," I was responsible for this work.

The electrician squad members were allowed to shower once a month, wearing just our wooden shoes. Rand would stand at the entrance to the shower and would evaluate how everyone looked. I was so skinny; it appeared that my skin was hanging off my bones. Rand stopped me and told me to come for a second helping of soup while he was feeding the servants of the block. The servants would sweep, rearrange the blankets and straighten out the barrack. He gave me second helpings

---

[28] Ohm's Law defines the relationship between voltage(V), current(I) and resistance(R).

of soup each day for a month. I am certain that Rand, whose first name I do not recall, saved my life.

Each morning, we electricians received one piece of bread to eat. At lunchtime we were given a watery soup with leaves, called Buna soup. The evening soup was different; it was slightly thicker, maybe with a little barley. Thankfully, Rand gave me second helpings of the evening soup. It took me a month to recover and I began looking better. I told him, "Thank you for helping me in my recovery." The Germans tracked what each person ate by marking down our tattoo number each time we were fed.

A few months later I received a secondary job. I would do this job after my regular work hours; I was assigned to clean the soup kettles. Scraping down the sides of the kettles, I made myself another serving of soup. Rand gave me that job because there was an opening; meaning, either someone had died or they were transferred, and he had pity on me. That job was mine for eight months, maybe more. I am almost certain this secondary job saved my life – again.

The Germans frequently ran a selection process to weed out the sickly-looking prisoners and send them off to the gas chambers. Rand saved the lives of about twenty prisoners by making healthier prisoners (me finally included) appear twice in front of the guards so that the sicklier prisoners did not have to step forward during the selection process. The sickly prisoners would have been immediately sent to their deaths had they appeared in front of the guards in their emaciated state.

One time in Buna, I came down with Krätze, know as Scabies in English, which caused scaly eruptions all over my skin. I was transferred to a special barrack on "Krätze Block." There everyone had Krätze. Those with Krätze still continued to report to work, but we had to return each night to the Krätze Block. Each night, the infected were given some kind of almond oil to rub onto our skin. This lasted for two weeks. Then, after two weeks, we were made to shower and sent back to our regular barracks.

When I finally returned to my barrack after recovering, I was given fresh underwear and a fresh uniform. By this time it was 1943 and the Eastern Front[29] at Stalingrad had fallen back under Russian control. The German army was struggling to maintain control of Eastern Europe. I heard this positive news from other prisoners, many of which had heard this from German prisoners. They spoke more freely with the German guards and non-Jewish prisoners.

One day after it rained, as I was traveling to work, I found a pair of leather shoes for myself – one black and one brown. It was easier to walk in leather shoes, but the soles were very thin. Once, while wearing these shoes, I stepped on a piece of wood with a rusty nail sticking out. The nail went right through the sole of the shoe and into my foot. I pulled out the rusty nail but a few days later I was unable to wear the shoes anymore because my foot was so swollen. I was worried about not being able to work and not being useful. It was very dangerous to be sick and not be able to walk or contribute. I had learned about the infirmary long before but I had never used it. I went there and met a Jewish doctor, Dr. Grossman from

---

[29] The Eastern Front was an arena of war between the European Axis states and Finland against the Soviet Union, Poland, and some other Allies-which encompassed Northern, Southern and Eastern Europe from June 22, 1941 to May 9, 1945.

Berlin, a prisoner like me. He looked at my foot and said that I was to be admitted and that he would need to operate. I was moved into the infirmary.

"Operate" was the word they used to describe cutting out dead flesh with no ointments or antibiotics and usually no anesthesia. There was no advanced medical care then – it was 1944 and I was in Auschwitz. They placed me on my back on a regular table and put a small rag on my face that contained a few drops of ether. I knew I had no choice because I needed my foot to heal in order to be useful again. For a short time I disappeared from planet Earth and from Auschwitz.

When I woke up, still under the influence of the ether, the orderlies told me there was roll call and the prisoners were yelling for everyone to get up. The orderlies were just having fun; there was no roll call and they were just teasing me. I had to jump on one leg to my bunk in the infirmary where I slept. We slept two to a bunk.

Two weeks later, the camp doctor came to visit. The doctor was the infamous Dr. Josef Mengele, also called the "Angel of Death." Mengele was best known for conducting life-threatening experiments on camp inmates. We had to stand facing him, naked, in front of our barrack. Dr. Grossman would stand next to him offering medical information. When it was my turn, I approached Dr. Mengele. My leg had already started healing and I tried my best to walk without a limp. Dr. Grossman did not wait for him to ask about my condition before he jumped in and said, "Oh, this youngster is going back to work tomorrow." If you could not work, your number was written down and you would be sent back to Birkenau, directly to the gas chambers. Without argument, Dr. Mengele agreed with Dr. Grossman. He gave me a slip of paper that allowed me to stay in the infirmary for two more days and then I was sent back to my barrack. Dr. Grossman saved my life.

I heard after the war that Dr. Grossman survived, as did Rand the Blokateste, but I never had the chance neither to see them again nor to thank them for all they did for me.

In the fall of 1944, allied forces sent air raids over Southern Poland. Bombs demolished the Buna Werke factory. Whenever there was an air raid alarm at our camp, the Nazis would not allow us to hide. They forced us to remain outside. So, I would lie on my back with a few of my friends from the same squad and watch the bombers fly over the factory. Many people were killed as the bombs fell but none who were near me. While we waited for death above, the Nazis hid in concrete bunkers.

Watching skyward, I would see a few rows of planes approach, dive and drop what looked like little bottles from the sky. By the time they reached the ground, the bombs were one-and-a-half meters long. They looked like they weighed about five hundred pounds. I watched the bombs split nearby buildings apart and then the huge power plant cooling tower went up in flames. A day after that bombing raid, the Germans made the surviving prisoners attempt to restore the buildings. Soon after, there was another air raid.

The third time the air raid alarms sounded, I raced into a bunker. The whole bunker was shaking when the bombs fell. As we sat safely inside, we could feel the vibrations passing through our bodies. A few other prisoners and some Germans were present in the bunker. At this point in the war, some of the Nazi guards became softer. I believed this happened because they felt that they were witnessing their own destruction. I felt happy, not because of the bunker over my head, but because of what the air raids destroyed. After the third air strike, there was nothing left standing.

Whoever was caught trying to escape the air raids was publicly hung at the roll call square as a warning in front of all the prisoners. At this point there were fifty barracks left, each holding two hundred prisoners. Before the air raids, the camp kitchen was powered by the power plant. With the power plant now destroyed, the remaining prisoners could not even get a little warm water for soup. All we had to eat were small pieces of bread.

The last air raid began Christmas, 1944.

Fortunately, the manufacturing facility never managed to produce one kilo of rubber nor one litre of fuel.

We heard giant guns roaring east of us. This was the Russian front coming closer to Buna. The Russians had already reached Krakow.

Then, in January 1945, the Germans liquidated Auschwitz. They forced us out of the camp before the Allied forces arrived. The Nazis told us that if we couldn't walk we should remain behind. I can't say how many stayed, but we were all scared that the Nazis would kill those who remained. We were ordered to take our blankets with us as we were forced to depart Buna.

The Death March to Gleiwitz II

January, 1945

Herded out of Buna-Monowitz, we walked westward. We were forced to march towards Germany.

I was beyond exhausted. My friends and I hooked arms to support each other. We were like sleepwalking zombies. Many people collapsed and were then shot as we continued to march.

The road was covered in a slippery snow, which dangerously glazed the bottom of my wooden shoes. I took off my shoes and walked barefoot. I walked part of the way like this. I did not want to have to slow down to get the snow off my feet. I did not even feel the cold. I felt like lying down somewhere, anywhere, to sleep because I felt so tired.

Those unable to walk any further were taken aside and shot on the spot. During the last fifty kilometers of this death march, we saw many hands and feet sticking out of the snow on the sides of the road. We walked more than one hundred kilometers. Farmers stood and watched us passing. Some laughed, as if we were criminals, people deserving of such cruel treatment. It showed that they did not care whatsoever. I don't remember their faces; it was such a struggle to keep going.

We continued forward, walking throughout the day and night and then a full day more, arriving that evening at Gleiwitz II, a distant part of Auschwitz. It was a small camp built for three thousand. All together we were now nine thousand prisoners.

When we arrived in the evening there was no room to lie down. There was not even room to sleep in the latrines. I found a piece of a wooden board, originally a washroom door, and I put it outside on the snow beside the entrance to the barrack.

The night was freezing. My friend Yankel Traube and I lied down side by side. We covered ourselves with the blankets we had taken from Buna-Monowitz. We said goodbye to each other, so certain we would never wake up again. We were so far beyond exhausted, immediately we slept.

When we woke up the next morning, not knowing what time it was and surprised to be alive, we were chased out of the camp again and to a waiting train. Yankel and I were separated in the chaos. There we were forced into roofless cars used for coal and gravel transport, approximately one hundred prisoners per car. We were forced in like geese in a cage. There was no room to lie down or even to sit. We had not eaten that morning before boarding the train. The last meal we had was a portion of bread several days earlier, prior to this long death march.

After many days of standing on the train with no food or water, the whole car seemed to be swaying like a wheat field due to my extreme exhaustion. I was feeling terribly weak; I fell down because I was sleeping while standing. Before I knew it, someone fell on top of me and I started choking, unable to breathe from the burden of his weight. I barely managed to push him off me. I believe many died this way – being pinned under those that collapsed.

Sometimes, the train stopped at railroad stations along the way but they never let us out. While stopped at a station, I saw an SS sergeant standing on a ramp with a weapon pointed at us. I asked him, "You want us to die on this train?" He replied, "No, we want to bring you to another camp."

The next station we arrived at was Matthausen concentration camp. I saw the camp on the hill and I felt so desperate to just get off the train. The Nazi leadership refused our entry and so our horrific journey continued. After the departure from Matthausen, people began to die more frequently. It felt like they lost all hope. I focused any energy I had into surviving each day. I cannot say why so many died and I did not.

We traveled in this open car for ten days without food, water, or access to toilets. The only thing we had to quench our thirst was the small amounts of snow that collected on our shoulders.

While the train traveled through Czechoslovakia, some kind Czechs would stand on bridges and throw food down into the cars to the lucky few able to reach these precious items. A friend I met up with after the war told me that he luckily caught a loaf of bread. He carefully hid his catch in his shirt and ate with careful attention to others. He feared someone might notice him and attack or possibly even kill him for the bread.

Due to three-quarters of the original passengers dying, there was a lot of room on the train during the final few days. Out of one hundred, only twenty-five people remained. We could no longer feel our hunger but we were incredibly thirsty, which is so much worse than hunger. Those of us who managed to survive were very sick and near death.

Finally we had arrived at a camp named Dora-Mittelbau, about 320 kilometers southeast of Berlin. We had travelled so far and suffered beyond any words I can manage to express. After passing through nearly 800 kilometers on the train the few who survived had arrived at Dora.

Dora-Mittelbau

January, 1945

Dora-Mittelbau was a labour camp that provided workers for the nearby Mittelwork V-2 rocket factory in Nordhausen. The camp was situated on the side of a mountain, while the rocket-building factory we worked at was actually built inside the mountain. There were two parallel tunnels running through the mountain for trains to come and go. There were also smaller side-tunnels connected to the two main tunnels.

Entrance to Dora-Mittlebau
Photo credit: German National Archives

When they opened up the side doors of the car, all inside who were alive were told to jump out. I hardly jumped; I collapsed over the side of the car onto the ground and I devoured the snow in an attempt to quench my thirst.

Had I arrived a year earlier to Dora-Mittelbau, I probably would not be here today. A year earlier, prisoners were building the tunnels with pressure hammers without any form of breathing protection from the dust. Dust would settle in the lungs and prisoners got tuberculosis very quickly and died. 60,000 prisoners were originally sent to Dora of whom 30,000 died.

I could no longer walk upright. I crawled on all fours all the way to the camp. Upon our arrival at Dora-Mittelbau, we slept on wood shavings in what was an old cinema. We had spent the first night and the next day there. I was given a piece of bread, which I hid in my shirt because I felt too ill and too exhausted to eat. When I woke up the next day, my bread was gone.

Inside the high fences at Dora, the camp was self-administrated by the kapos, or German criminals. The treatment we Jews received from these people, our fellow prisoners, was unimaginable. They stole our food – they were stealing food from the starving! When there was a death in the block, these cruel kapos didn't announce it. They hid the body so they would have one more portion of food! Once there were another few deaths, after a day or two of eating the rations of the dead, they would present the dead bodies, wait and again do the same.

When food was brought in it was given to these criminals to distribute and they never divided it fairly. At Dora I was constantly starving.

Assigned to an electricians working squad, I worked with my friend Moishe Brownfeld. We were partners. The work was very complicated. I was tasked with changing motors, electrical switches, and wiring. Dora was a horrible camp and I was very lucky that I worked inside without the constant intimidation of a German kapo. My boss was a kind, simple man, an employee from a town near Dora. He did not treat me so poorly.

Being inside the tunnels, I felt very fortunate with my job assignment. There were many prisoners that had to carry heavy machinery outside in the freezing cold. Later in the spring, these same unfortunate men had to walk in slippery mud up to their ankles. Those who slipped in the mud could expect a savage beating from the guards. The guards did not care whatsoever how many of us died; they just wanted their rockets built. Eventually, the rockets were launched towards London off the shores of Calais,

France. The rockets we were forced to build destroyed half the city.

Occasionally, as prisoners returned to the camp from work, there would be a hanging. The Nazis claimed that prisoners had sabotaged some work or project and deserved to be hanged. They did this to keep our terror alive.

In our barracks, we were forced to sleep three people to a bunk. Each bunk was approximately one hundred centimeters, or forty inches, wide. Each day our rations became smaller at Dora. During the last few weeks of work we did not even get a piece of bread. An unpeeled mini potato was all we received and most of the time it was rotten. I was starving so I ate the rotten potatoes without hesitation.

The workers at the factory were either prisoners like me or German civilians due to the top-secret nature of the factory. One day, our civilian German foreman approached and asked me, "Young boy, what did you do? Why are you a prisoner?" I did not know what to reply, so I said, "Because I am Jewish." He turned away abruptly in disbelief and he separately asked my friend Moishe the same question. Of course, the foreman was given the same answer. After those two brief discussions, the foreman became friendlier towards us. In order to not be seen directly helping us, he hid small pieces of bread and would tell us where to find them. I used to walk around the whole plant near the rocket assembly line to uncover the hidden bread.

Back in Auschwitz we had come into contact with non-German civilian workers – Poles, Ukrainians, Frenchmen and Yugoslavians. We would try and make deals with them by trading some clothing or underwear for food and sometimes for money. Moishe had two marks (German currency) that he brought with him from Auschwitz.

Moishe approached our foreman and told him that he had found two marks. He was afraid to mention that he had smuggled them into the camp, and Moishe asked the foreman if he could buy some bread from him with the money. The naïve foreman replied, "If you found some money, someone must have lost it." Concerned, he went to the SS administration and reported that a prisoner found two marks. I do not believe it ever occurred to him how serious a crime the Nazis would consider this. They told him to send the prisoner to the administration office. Two marks would have been worth approximately fifty cents. My friend would likely be hanged over fifty cents.

They called Moishe's prisoner number over the intercom speakers that were heard all over the camp. Moishe did not have any choice but to go to the administration office. When he got there, the SS beat him severely and asked where he got the marks. Whatever he told them they would say, "It's not true, you stole the money!" His whole face was bleeding and bruised. One of the SS men then asked what they should do with him. Another SS man said, "They are hanging some Russians at roll call; let's hang him too."

I was standing at roll call and watched everything. Indeed, there were Russians being hanged. I saw the Russians dangling from their necks, hands and feet bound together.

Moishe was dragged by his neck and made to stand next to the gallows near the hanging dead. Suddenly, at the same time, we heard air raid alarms. The intercom blared, "Please disperse yourselves and hide!" Moishe dispersed with everyone else and hid. The whole incident with the money was forgotten.

Many years after liberation, I ran into Moishe Brownfield in Israel at the Dead Sea. I was thrilled to see him. Standing in the healing and densely salted water, I heard a familiar voice behind me. When I turned around, I saw Moishe! He told me that I was the only survivor he knew that witnessed his "almost hanging." He had a brother who survived and another brother fortunate to have already been in Palestine throughout the war. Moishe and I remain friends to this day.

Two weeks after this incident, our foreman started telling stories about how the Nazis "are finished." He named cities that were bombed and destroyed and said thousands of civilians had died. I tried not to react to his stories, good or bad. My instincts told me to just listen and to not say anything.

I don't even want to believe that I was at this camp and went through all I went through in Dora-Mittelbau. The kapos were all German prisoners; there were no Jewish kapos. At least in Auschwitz there were many Jewish kapos and many were decent people. In Dora, there was so much violence, so much brutality, that people were constantly being murdered. There was always a backlog of bodies piled high for the crematoria.

In retrospect, Dora was worse than Auschwitz and it wasn't even a death camp as Auschwitz was; it was a work camp! There were SS men present at Dora with their vicious dogs but they had very little daily presence there. They stayed in a separate portion of the camp and they only came into the heart of the camp for roll call or other political matters.

In April 1945, after nearly four months at Dora-Mittlebau, the Germans transported the remaining prisoners to Bergen-Belsen.

Bergen-Belsen and the End of the War

April, 1945

Bergen-Belsen was a concentration camp that began to house more and more Jews as the Germans lost control of Eastern Europe. By 1945 there were about 60,000 Jewish prisoners held there. The camp was originally designed for only 10,000 prisoners. Due to the overpopulation, many died of sickness from diseases like typhus.

On the first day of Passover, April 1st, 1945, we all stood at the roll call square of Dora-Mittelbau. The Germans separated the Jews from non-Jews. My group received a mini loaf of bread to share among us and we were swiftly chased into open railroad cars; the same open cars used to transport V-2 rockets. SS guards sat on the bumpers in between each car to ensure nobody escaped. As we traveled, we passed railroad stations with idle trains in flames.

The Germans kept us on the cars sitting under a tarp without water, food, or any kind of a toilet, not even a bucket. One man had diarrhea and every few minutes he would go to the bumper to relieve himself. Without warning, an SS officer shot him and watched him fall from the train to the tracks below. Although the station we arrived at, Belsen, was only approximately 200 kilometers north of Dora-Mittlebau, the journey to Bergen-Belsen took approximately five days. I believe this was due to the destruction of German railway lines and the state of the many stations. The train also seemed to stop at each station we passed.

Eventually, we marched from Belsen station to the camp we were assigned to; an empty army camp, north of Bergen-Belsen. First, we were delivered to the SS administration building, but there were no SS present. The main camp was a kilometer from the building. Whoever was unable to walk was unhesitatingly shot and killed.

When I arrived at this camp, I saw two young prisoners running into the basement of a two-storey army building. I followed them blindly into this basement. I was shocked to find myself in a dark room filled one-foot-deep with raw potatoes. It was becoming hugely overcrowded, filled with starving prisoners trying to take potatoes.

I was so skinny I easily managed to crouch in between people's legs. I grabbed a few potatoes, snuck them away in my shirt and rushed to find a way out. Behind me, the staircase was jammed with countless prisoners pushing forward, desperate to get out. I saw a small open window that seemed far too high up for me to reach, but I knew without reaching it I would be crushed to death. I do not recall how, but somehow it seemed I became superman and flew out the window! I suspect someone behind me gave me a boost, which helped to free me from this room so dangerously packed with the starving.

One could not eat raw potatoes and there was no way to boil them, but one of my friends had matches. We found some pieces of wood and a can and made a makeshift grater by punching holes in the can with a nail we found. We grated the potatoes and put them in another can with some water. We lit a little fire with the wood and matches and boiled the potatoes. Three of my friends and I sat down in a circle and ate our soup one spoonful at a time. I got to use two spoons because after all, we were eating my potatoes.

For the next two weeks, there was no distribution of food and people were starving. We had water but I believe the water was polluted and so many people were dying. Late one evening, one of the Jewish boys started screaming that he heard tanks coming. He had heard the rumbling of nearby British military tanks invading Germany. We started running towards the fence to catch a glimpse of the tanks but the guards, Hungarian soldiers, would not allow this. We resigned to our barracks to sleep.

The next morning, April 15, 1945, at roll call, fifteen high-ranking SS men arrived and ordered us to form lines and rows to be counted. These officers arrived with white armbands, which I realized was significant. Something was going to change but I was unsure what this might be. I didn't believe in miracles, so, after all the suffering, the countless deaths I had witnessed, the fear that my family was wiped away by this terror, I could not be certain of anything. The column of tanks from the day before could be a sign of liberation, but was I prepared to believe this? I was only aware that white meant surrender in times of war.

Within minutes of the onset of roll call several non-SS military vehicles entered the camp. We realized immediately that they were not German military. They were the British military police, rapidly approaching during our final roll call. The British military quickly disarmed all the guards and the German SS. No prisoners were allowed to harm or have contact with the SS or the guards. The remaining Nazis were loaded onto British military jeeps and driven off. The Hungarian guards remained to guard the prison gates.

I will try to describe what happened next, but it was truly an event beyond belief. From all corners of the camp, prisoners emerged from their hiding spots wielding their own national flags. I have no idea how they got such flags. Everyone was hugging each other. Not only had we survived, we would finally be liberated.

Immediately the sun seemed to shine brighter. I felt free. After so many years of being tormented as a slave and as a prisoner to the Nazis, I felt numb, frozen. I did not know how to react, to be happy or sad. When I heard of the possible number of Jews killed I could not grasp what I had learned. Was it truly possible that the numbers were in the millions? I could not imagine that it was possible that I had lost my entire family. I did not want to believe my family was gone.

Reflection came slowly. I thought for sure I would meet my parents or some of my relatives but I was not too hopeful. I couldn't think much about the future, just about finding a way to sustain myself. I knew we were liberated but I was starving and I knew I had to find food and find the power to regain my strength to sustain my life before I could face the future.

I did not laugh. I did not cry. But my heart ached for a long time.

Liberation!

April, 1945

At liberation I stood 170 centimeters (five feet and seven-and-a-half inches) tall, and weighed 31.7 kilograms (seventy pounds). I was twenty-two years old, clinging to life by a thread after being enslaved and malnourished for so many years.

There were a few thousand survivors liberated from Bergen-Belsen, however, we had no food or means for survival. The rations they gave us were a very small amount of pork schmaltz[30] and powdered milk. People died from these small rations because their bodies couldn't absorb the fat after so many years of starvation. It took two more weeks until proper aid was distributed. In the meantime, many starved. Many survivors also died during this time from sickness, exhaustion, as well as from starvation. We were walking zombies.

I managed to eat the schmaltz and drink the powdered milk but it did little to sustain me. There is a rule in Jewish dietary law that allows the consumption of non-kosher foods in times of desperation, so although it was pork schmaltz, I felt it was okay to eat.

The second day after our liberation, a British ambulance arrived. Rabbi Levine, a military chaplain emerged and stood on a roof to pray with us. We all stood around him as he spoke. He said that his first prayer would be Shehecheyanu[31], a prayer for renewal to strengthen the remaining survivors. He told us we should

---

[30] Rendered pork fat.

[31] A traditional Jewish prayer to celebrate new, unusual or special occasions.

be happy because one kilometer away was a camp of tens of thousands of dead prisoners, referring to the main camp of Bergen-Belsen. Angered by his words, our response was simple, "If they are all dead, then they don't need anything. We are alive and we must eat."

The Rabbi told us to have patience. This was an almost impossible feat for us survivors. In our state, the waiting was life threatening. For a short while after liberation the remaining survivors acted a little wildly, almost crazed, having been starved for years. We were free now and we wanted and genuinely needed immediate care.

It took time to grasp the enormity of the crimes of the Nazis. Waiting for food did not seem moral or just, and there was no time to waste as we were starving to death as we waited for this relief. We also could not grasp the British military's lack of reverence for our dead. When the British arrived at the main camp of Bergen-Belsen, they discovered tens of thousands of dead bodies strewn all over the camp grounds. We watched the British use bulldozers to force thousands of our dead into mass graves. It seemed criminal. We expected the disrespect for our dead of the Nazis, and we could not understand that a crime like this might continue after liberation. We could not comprehend the shocking number of dead bodies, nor the tactical difficulty in dealing with so many dead. There was seemingly no other solution to manage so many corpses.

Sign erected by the British liberators outside Bergen-Belsen.
Photo circa 1945.

Soon after witnessing the bulldozers, the British set Bergen-Belsen on fire with flamethrowers to prevent the spread of disease.

No survivor had showered in weeks. We did nothing all day but spend every moment of time scavenging for food within the camp. Some people escaped the camp; the British allowed the Hungarian guards to stay behind to watch over us. The guards would still shoot at those who tried to escape. A few survivors died after liberation at the hands of the Hungarian guards but some made it out to neighboring farms to beg for food.

Finally, after two weeks, we received rations from Jewish Relief Organizations out of London and from UNRRA[32]. The American Jewish Joint Distribution Committee from New York also sent supplies.

I later learned that the SS Komendant from Bergen-Belsen, Josef Kramer, was tried by the British and hanged along with other officers after the Belsen Trial of

---

[32] The United Nations Relief and Rehabilitation Administration; an international relief agency representing 44 countries that operated from 1943 – 1947.

September 1945. I went with friends to the court gallery to attend the trials. There were such stupid questions posed by the British judges, like "how long was the stick he would hit you with?" These questions seemed so ridiculous, so trivial.

The remaining survivors of our group numbered approximately two thousand, all men. Worried about disease such as typhus and lice, the British came back into the camp and fumigated the remaining people with DDT[33]. We all had lice and we survivors remained fearful to resist, plus we had no idea about the dangers of DDT.

The British then put us on trucks and sent us fifty kilometers south to a town called Celle. It was the intention of the British to make a hospital out of the Bergen Belsen military base that we were leaving behind.

---

[33] Dichlorodiphenyltrichloroethane: a chemical pesticide.

Recovery at Celle

May, 1945

All the barely living survivors from Bergen-Belsen were moved to the camp in Celle. I finally received proper rations and I recovered quickly.

All the survivors were so hungry we wanted to eat everything that was offered. However, I realized I must be careful because my digestive system was not used to processing a normal amount of food. Many prisoners died shortly after the liberation due to diarrhea and complications from overeating after so many years of starvation.

After being in Celle for a few months, I joined a religious group of Jews. I felt that the religious people were friendlier than the others and we, in groups of five or six, went out to visit the mayors of surrounding towns to request aid. In this way we saw the German countryside. We behaved like teenagers, traveling by coal train, finally free to be young; to be boys. We managed to get some food coupons by group appeal to the heads of small towns. We also got some Bezugschein[34], special paper slips that allowed us to obtain clothes. After acquiring new clothes the Germans instructed us to give back our prisoner uniforms. Looking back, returning my terrible uniform was a mistake; I should have kept this outfit as a token of remembrance or a museum piece for the future. At the time, I wanted more than anything to be done with the memories and pain associated with my uniform.

Once, my friends and I found a deserted cookie factory where there was a large amount of cookie dough

---

[34] Post-war paper merchandising coupons used for obtaining clothing and sundry home goods.

piled on the floor. Nobody seemed to know what to do with it so I quickly grabbed what I could and brought it back to a baker I knew. My baker friend diluted the dough and baked a cake, our first since long before the war.

Recently, during December 2007 in Florida, I ran into a man named Meyer Steinmetz, a Romanian Jew. After noticing his number tattoo, we began to talk. Apparently, he was also at Celle and we reminisced about our experiences and about the old cookie factory.

I stayed in Celle for a couple of months. Time was spent mindlessly exploring the German countryside. Staying didn't do anything for us so we decided to go to Hanover. A friend had just returned from Hanover and suggested there was more to see and explore from there, so we went forward.

Henry Melnick

Henry at age 23 during the summer of 1945

Hela's Story

August, 1945

During late summer 1945, I left Celle with my friends to move to the bigger city of Hanover. We hitchhiked the whole way on every kind of transportation – on open coal cars, automobiles, horse and buggy; any way we could find to move forward, we did. In Hanover we rented a small, clean room with three beds from a German family. We paid very little for the room.

Hanover's Jewish population was now only 1,000 after the war. The population before the war was 4,800 and only 100 survived hidden within the city. The transitional community was much larger. I found work with the town Jewish Committee and I became a supplier of food for the Jews who came from the east as survivors of the Holocaust as well as for the many returning from Russia. I witnessed many Jews who boarded illegal ships trying to reach Palestine.

My friends and I often took time off to visit surrounding cities and towns. There, again, we would appeal to the mayors of these towns for their support of the surviving Jews. We asked them because we felt they owed us. We would tell them our stories and they would run away like children. They sometimes even gave us money to make us disappear like the bad memories we invoked in them.

Once, I traveled with several friends to Hamburg. Not far from the central railroad station a young gentile-looking girl approached us. She was wearing a sweater with a cross on the back and shoes with wooden soles. She said she overheard us speaking Yiddish, a language that was familiar to her. She asked if we were Jewish and we told her we were. She explained to us that she was Jewish, too, and her name was Hela.

We could not believe she was Jewish. She did not look Jewish. She had brown hair and very green eyes. She looked Polish and spoke without an accent. One of my friends had a prayer book in his pocket. In order for Hela to prove herself, he gave his prayer book to her to read. She read it out loud with no problems!

She told us she came to Hamburg from a displaced persons camp in the north. She was in Hamburg to get to the Red Cross in order to send letters to one of her three brothers, Charles. Charles was studying at the Polytechnic School in Paris where he safely remained during the war. She began recounting her story of survival to us:

Hela Sosnowicz lived with her family in Warsaw when the Germans invaded Poland. Together with the Jews of Warsaw, her family was captured and ordered to live within the Warsaw Ghetto. The second oldest in Hela's family, her brother David, had many business connections. The Sosnowicz family manufactured clothing for children. Through their family business,

David had a good relationship with a Christian Polish family outside of the Warsaw Ghetto walls. David was a member of the Shomer Hatzair[35] before the war and was an activist in the underground movement ŻOB[36]. In 1943, he became an active member of the Warsaw Ghetto Uprising.

Fearing the worst, David asked the Christian family if they would be willing to help save his sister Hela. The lady of the house, Mrs. Kwiatkowski, agreed and told David to send Hela to them. David then had to bribe a policeman at the ghetto entryway. Hela left her ghetto building with a folded up piece of paper in her hand. She presented this paper to the guard at the gate and he let her through.

Heart beating out of her chest, Hela departed from the ghetto and was temporarily accepted into the Kwiatkowskis' family home. Mr. Kwiatkowski traveled to a small town where Polish families kept their birth

---

[35] A Socialist–Zionist youth movement founded in 1913 in Galicia, Austria-Hungary.

[36] Żydowska Organizacja Bojowa; the Jewish Combat Organization.

certificates with the Church. He generously went to the priest and bought the birth certificate of a deceased Polish girl to give to Hela. Hela Sosnowicz suddenly became Helena Kaminska.

Hela traveled to Warsaw city hall with her picture and the birth certificate Mr. Kwiatkowski purchased to arrange for a proper identification card, which she received that very day. She worked to forget her real name, Hela Sosnowicz, until the war was over. If her real identity were known, Hela would have been captured and sent to the camps or killed. She was forced to conceal any Yiddish or Hebrew knowledge and to speak perfect Polish so that her Jewish identity would remain hidden. One simple slip and Hela's life would have ended.

Hela rarely lived in the Kwiatkowski family's home unless in grave danger. If the Germans ever caught her there, they would have immediately killed Hela and the entire Kwiatkowski family. The family took tremendous personal risk to save Hela. She attempted to avoid further risk to these generous people. To this end, she initially lived with some old non-Jewish Polish women in the basement of a building.

The Kwiatkowski family had a daughter, Christina, and together with "Helena" they would go out in the streets. One time, a German patrol officer approached them and Christina quickly told "Helena" to tie up her shoelace so that she would not have to look into the German's eyes.

Several times, while on her own, "Helena" was approached by German patrols and other Poles. Several times, Polish citizens recognized her as a Jew from before the war. Each time they would take something from her in exchange for keeping her identity a secret. One time someone took her watch, another time a ring, and so on.

Once, while walking on the street, Hela's worst fears came true. A Pole recognized her as a Jew and reported her presence to some nearby German officers. Moments later, Hela noticed the SS officers racing behind. Key in hand, she ran straight back to the basement where she lived.

She was lucky that the Polish women she lived with were not yet home. The officers knocked on the door; she could hear the neighbors screaming that a Jewish girl had run into the building. She ignored their banging and had taken the key out of the keyhole so that no one would suspect there was anyone inside. They blew at the door so loudly, almost as loud as she felt her heart was pounding in her chest. Eventually, they left. She knew that sooner or later they would return, so she had to find a new hiding spot immediately.

There was a streetcar that travelled out of Warsaw to Otwock and back. Otwock was a resort town where Poles went to spend quiet days on balconies that overlooked the Vistula river. It was popular with Jews in the summertime before the war and became a place of refuge for Hela during the daytime. So terrified that someone would recognize her again, Hela spent whole days sitting on verandas in empty cottages. In the evenings she returned to Warsaw and slept.

The Kwiatkowski family arranged for her to find another place to sleep in Warsaw, on a street called

Vengerska. She began working at a factory, sewing men's shirts for a prominent company named Opus. Nobody bothered her at this job. No one ever suspected she was Jewish. Her Polish was perfect without any trace of an accent.

When Hela asked the Kwiatkowski family why they agreed to assist her and took such great risk in the face of severe repercussions from the Nazis, Mrs. Kwiatkowski recounted that during the war, Hela's mother Batia had appeared to her in a dream pleading with her to save Hela's life.

April 1943, the Warsaw Ghetto Uprising began. Hela could see the ghetto in flames from the streets of Warsaw. She thought of her brother David fighting in the ghetto. Hela felt helpless; she could do nothing for fear of exposing her identity. After the uprising, David was sent to Treblinka, a death camp in Poland, and there he was murdered by the Nazis.

Near the end of 1943, before Christmas, the Opus factory administrators demanded that each woman who worked in the factory get a note from a priest proving they had attended confession. In exchange, the women would each receive a Christmas gift. Most of the women refused, saying that they did not need a gift for Christmas. Mr. Kwiatkowski advised Hela to further strengthen her Christian identity, and said, "Let these women not go to confession, but you yourself should still go."

So, Hela went to confession. She told the priest that she had had a disagreement with her mother. He gave her a blessing and a note. She went to church and listened to heinous anti-Semitism from Trzeciak, a Catholic Priest, infamous for his anti-Semitic vigor who relentlessly advocated killing all Jews. For Hela, living this double life was harder than being a prisoner at a camp. The constant fear, the uncertainty, and the incessant waiting to be discovered were excruciatingly painful and her angst never ended.

At her new home on Vengerska Street, Hela met two sisters in the building and befriended them until liberation. She lived in their building for a few months while working at the Opus factory.

During the summer of 1944, there was a Polish uprising against the Germans to liberate Warsaw. The uprising was organized by the Armia Krajowa[37]. Unfortunately, the uprising was unsuccessful. The Germans foiled the uprising and bombed the city – building after building – destroying absolutely everything. They sent many of the general population of Warsaw to concentration camps in Germany. Hela and her two friends were sent to Sachsenhausen-Oranienburg[38], then later to Bergen-Belsen, and finally to a camp I believe was called Kleinmachnow. In all these camps Hela maintained her identity as a political non-Jewish Polish prisoner. Hela spent a total of a few months at these camps. The Poles were not treated much differently from the Jewish prisoners at this point in the war.

Hela was liberated at a small military base north of Hamburg and eventually she arrived at a displaced persons camp near Hanover.

---

[37] The Polish Resistance Army.

[38] A concentration camp for political prisoners.

Hela's parents were liquidated from the Warsaw Ghetto during the summer of 1942, removed to the famous Umschlagplatz[39]. Approximately 300,000 Jews were liquidated and deported to Treblinka, the extermination camp. There, all were murdered upon arrival.

---

[39] A ramp in the Warsaw Ghetto and the collection and deportation point to Treblinka.

Hela and Henry in Hanover

August, 1945

I asked Hela to return with us to Hanover. I had my eye on her. She was a beautiful Jewish woman with a nice figure, but it wasn't just a physical attraction. Every one of us boys wanted to save a Jewish soul by bringing her among fellow Jews. Hela had been isolated for so long. Until meeting us, she believed she was the only Jew left in the entire world. We told her there were still a few thousand surviving Jews from Bergen-Belsen. We told her to join us right away but she refused to come with us back to Hanover. She hesitated only because she had sent letters to her brother, Charles, in Paris with a return address of the camp from where she was liberated. She did not know if Charles had even survived and did not want to abandon hope of getting his response at her camp.

We gave Hela some time to think about it and told her that if she decided to come with us, she should meet us the next day at the same place at the same time. Sure enough, she returned. We all hitchhiked via cars and trains, sitting on coal cars, or whatever other means we could manage to return to Hanover. We had a few German marks we received from the mayors of several towns we visited. This was enough to buy some food for our journey. Within a month, Hela and I became engaged.

We used to travel together to Bergen Belsen where there was a cinema converted to a synagogue. We would attend services there for Rosh Hashanah and Yom Kippur during 1945 and 1946. We had an engagement party in the fall of 1945 in a restaurant. The girls baked all kinds of cakes.

On February 12th, 1946, Hela and I were married in Hanover. Hela, which translates to Chaya in Hebrew, was also my mother's first name. In Jewish custom, one should not marry a woman with the same name as one's mother. However, a rabbi in Germany told me that I was allowed to marry Hela since my mother was no longer living. Even though I was not positive they were dead, I knew my parents were sent to Bełżec, so it was very unlikely that they survived.

On the day we were to marry, I fell ill. I was too sick to stand and we resolved to see a doctor before the wedding ceremony. We thought of postponing the wedding but the rabbi said that once you set a wedding date, you cannot postpone it.

Hela went with me to the doctor's office. The doctor told me that I was afflicted with a serious infection that attacked my whole body. While passing by us in the waiting room, the doctor announced, "This girl is marrying a dead man today." Somehow I regained my strength quickly and went with Hela to the Rabbi to perform the wedding ceremony.

Engagement photo of Hela, 20, and Henry, 22, in February, 1945

To make the wedding "kosher" we needed another married couple to act as witnesses. Of course, at that point, our friends were not married; and of course we did not have anyone except each other. As we looked down to the street from the window, we saw a young man and a young woman walking together on the street. My friend Tsvi Wilczek asked them if they were Jewish. In Yiddish he shouted down to them, "Are you of the tribe?" After answering yes, Tsvi asked them, "Are you married?" to which the man replied, "It's none of your business!" After explaining the situation we asked them to be our witnesses. That married couple, Renia and Morris Steinhorn, became our closest friends. Morris and I remained close until his death from cancer, and to this day, I remain very close to his wife Renia.

Henry Melnick

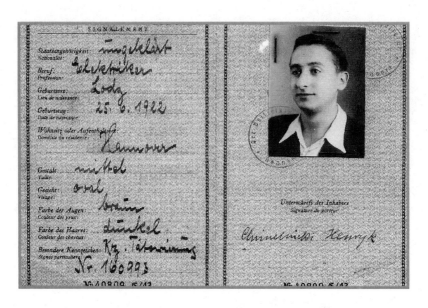

Henry's German-issued passport, 1946

Life together after the war

In Hanover, Hela and I enjoyed attending different shows together – the opera, some theatre and the symphony. We tried to stay busy at all times. We tried not to think too much about the past, instead looking straight ahead only towards the future. We had no choice. It was hard going from being treated like an animal, a slave, to having complete freedom, having enough to sustain oneself, feeling appreciated and loved. For some time we felt very unsettled.

We rented a nice sized room from a German evangelic family on the third floor of a building at 15 Veckenstrasse

Street, one of the main streets of Hanover looking toward Lindon Street.

At this time we also managed to establish lines of communication with Hela's two surviving brothers. Charles, the eldest, and Meir, the youngest, kept in touch through mailed letters. Charles survived in France as part of the Charles de Gaulle underground army and Meir survived through Auschwitz and many other camps. He was liberated in Theresienstadt, both a ghetto and a concentration camp.

While in Hanover I continued to work for the Jewish Committee, supplying food to the new Jewish immigrants to Germany arriving from the east, mostly from Poland and Russia. We all immigrated because there was so much uncertainty and anti-Semitism breaking out throughout Eastern Europe. Germany allowed a chance for all refugees to register to go to the United States, Canada, or to attempt to make it to Palestine. There was constant discrimination and the Jewish refugees desperately wanted to be part of the free world.

The Jewish Committee would house the immigrants in one of two refugee camps in Hanover. One of the refugee camps was on Spinosa Street and another was on Bittner Street. There, the immigrants would remain for a few days and then they would head south, many attempting to obtain entry into Palestine, regardless of legality. Others would travel to Italy, France, or elsewhere in the hopes of escaping the anti-Semitism they continued to experience in Poland.

In the summer of 1947 it was our turn. We left illegally for Palestine, which was still not a recognized country. We were led illegally to a place to pass through the border to Belgium in Aachen, Germany. From there, we would continue through the border from Belgium to France, to finally arrive at a port in Sète. All this would be done in order to board a ship called the Exodus. However, we did not arrive at the Exodus in time. In fact, we could not make it past the German-Belgian border. The border was supposed to be simple to pass through because the guards were bribed to let our transport through. However, there was an unexpected change of guards and our plans were foiled.

We later found out that the Exodus did not successfully arrive in Palestine. Denied entry by the British, the ship was forcedly returned to the port in Hamburg, Germany.

It felt to us like we were required to take one step backwards in order to take two steps into the future. We made our way to Düsseldorf and spent a few weeks there. The Jewish community in West Germany supported us. The British, having been alerted to our attempt to illegally escape to Palestine, attempted to place us in a refugee camp somewhere near Dusseldorf. However, we were desperate to return to our friends and our many connections in Hanover. There were many Ukrainians placed in the Dusseldorf refugee camp and we were doubtful of their backgrounds. Were they former Ukrainian police? Were they dangerous towards us? We could not know because we didn't have any relationships or any connections there.

A gentleman from the Jewish Community Organization arranged railroad tickets for our return to Hanover. Because the British had learned of our deceit and they wanted to detain us for attempting to leave illegally, we were told to pull the train's emergency brakes before the train arrived at the station in Hanover and to "disappear." So, just before the train maneuvered into the station we pulled the emergency brakes and ran down the levy to an embankment to hide. The German passengers on board could not understand what was going on. We heard the remark, "Where are they going? There is no station here!" When the British learned that the Jews they were looking for were on the train, they waited at the station to round us up, but by the time the train finally pulled in we were well on our way into the city.

The leaders of the Jewish Brigade were running the whole illegal emigration scheme. These leaders were able to go to Hanover Station to watch how the British were checking German documentation in order to help us to maintain our safety. When we returned to our original apartment, the owners said, "Why are you back? We thought you were going to France?" to this we replied, "Not France, Frankfurt!" The owners were not Jews and we could not trust them with news of the failure of our journey.

In 1948, after spending three post-war years in Germany and recovering much of our strength and determination, we finally received official certificates from the United Nations. These certificates allowed us, as part of a party of 10,000 Jews, to travel legally to Palestine. The UN allowed these departures once each month for ten months.

After preparing to leave Hanover, we made our way and were among the first to arrive at a transit camp named Bocholt in West Germany. From there, we crossed the German-French border by train and ended up in Marseille, France, which borders on the Mediterranean Sea.

Charles, Hela, Henry and Meir walking arm in arm through Marseille, France, January 1948, on their way to Palestine.

When we arrived in Marseille and got off the train, we met up with Charles and Meir, Hela's two surviving brothers.

A few days after our arrival in Marseille, we bid farewell to Charles and Meir, and Hela and I boarded a small Romanian passenger ship called Transylvania. After several uneasy days we happily arrived in Haifa. It appeared beautiful and picturesque. The British greeted us at the port and welcomed us into Palestine.

A New Life in Israel

February, 1948

In the Port of Haifa, we were brought to the bus station and boarded an armored bus that was very hot and full to capacity. Halfway to Tel Aviv, we drove along a section of road surrounded by Arab villages. These Arab villagers were not friendly to Jews. At one point on the journey through Israel, many Arabs shot at our bus. The whole bus was thickly armored with a small port hole so those responsible for transporting us could see out. We had an armed guard on board for our protection. He returned fire with his Sten[40] gun through a slit in the armor, and we continued on our way. We stopped for a short time in Zikhron Ya'akov where we changed buses, and the rest of the way to Tel Aviv was thankfully safe.

I had no idea what Tel Aviv would be like. Upon our arrival I was shocked to see neon signs in windows with Hebrew letters. Looking back, it was a beautiful sight after all we had been through, but at the time I could not see the beauty because it was totally overwhelming and a completely new start for us, all alone. We were strangers in Israel; the only people we knew were Hela's third cousins. We spoke Yiddish, not Hebrew, so this fresh start was very difficult. The Jewish Agency placed Hela and I at the Commercial Hotel on Levinsky Street in Tel Aviv. We were there for a couple of weeks, during which we went out and explored the city. Afterwards, we were told that we had to manage on our own.

We moved from the hotel into a Jewish-owned shack across Yafo, known in English as Jaffa. In Yafo, there

---

[40] A British submachine gun.

was constant shooting day and night between Arabs and Jews. We frequently visited Hela's third cousins, spending our evenings in Tel Aviv. Upon returning to our shack we would crawl on all fours to avoid being shot!

After a short while I enrolled in the Israeli Defense Forces. I was issued a gun and finally we felt safer. In 1948, Hela became pregnant. During the Israeli War of Independence I participated in the fight to free up the road from Tel Aviv to Jerusalem. I was a proud member of the Hativa Sheva, the 7th Armored Brigade.

**Insignia of the Israeli Defense Forces
Hativa Sheva (7th Armored Brigade)**

At this time, there were three Jewish military armies operating in Palestine; the Haganah; the main Jewish military organization, the Etzel Irgun, Menachim Begin's military party and the Stern Group, also known as Lehi, which the English called the Stern Group Bandits. On May 26, 1948, 12 days after Israel's declaration of independence was signed, Defense Minister David Ben Gurion announced that there must be one undivided army for Israel. Combining the Haganah, the Etzel and Lehi, he named it the Tzva Haganah LeYisrael, meaning Israel Defense Forces or IDF, which remains in place today. I recall these events like they were yesterday.

On June 21, 1948, I participated in a historic event known as the Altalena Affair. A ship named the Altalena arrived in Tel Aviv carrying a large cache of weapons from France. Disagreement between the IDF and remnants of the Etzel about what to do with the weapons led to a brief but violent confrontation on the beach. After the IDF seized the cargo, I helped unload the weapons off the ship. Eventually the Altalena was fired upon and sunk off the coast of Tel Aviv.

Altalena Memorial on Tel Aviv beach

Grateful for my new sense of belonging and my freedom, I actively participated in the actual building of the Burma Road to enable critical supplies to reach Jerusalem during the war of independence. Ben Dunkelman was my commander in this brigade.

Once other roads were opened, we were sent to the Galilee in northern Israel and stationed at a camp called Machane 80 (Base 80). There, I met the Jewish police member from Tarnów, the man who surrendered my friend Moishe and I to the SS after he found us hiding in a basement. This, of course, led to our liquidation to the Szebnie concentration camp. I felt I had to report this to the commander of his unit. The commander took both of us to Netanya, to the commission where Nazis and their accomplices were tried.

We both shared our perspectives. He apologized and was released since I did not have witnesses to back up my claims. The court ruled that he was not guilty because although he did catch me and turn me in, he did not kill me. However, my friend Moishe Leizer Bergman was also caught at the same time and he was killed shortly after his arrival in Auschwitz. Moishe Leizer was a very smart young man, and his loss was tremendous. He wrote poetry and he wrote about all the camps and his experiences. He had his writings with him when he was taken to the gas chambers. He was 19 years old. Unfortunately, the Commission did not take the loss of Moishe Leizer into consideration while making their decision.

On September 17, 1948, Hela gave birth to our son. We named him after my father, Elijah.

During my last few months of army service I worked as an electrician in a military garage. Over this time, I learned a great deal about auto electric service. In the summer of 1949, I was released from the army. Shortly after, I opened my own auto electric shop called Start Auto Electric in Tel Aviv.

On June 16, 1953, we were blessed with our daughter, named after Hela's mother, Batia.

In 1965, after raising our family in Israel for 17 years, Hela, the children and I moved to Toronto, Canada.

I have no regrets for any of the choices we made – moving to Israel, joining the army, creating a life for our family in Israel, then eventually moving to Canada with our children and starting over yet again. I have no regrets.

Present Day in Toronto – In my own words

Much has happened, good and bad, over forty-four years in Canada.

I was devastated by the loss of my wife Hela in 1987. I married Elaine in 1991 and we remain happily together to this day.

Start Auto Electric is still open for business. Of course, the business was relocated to downtown Toronto and even now, I still work at Start.

Elijah and Batia have given me much joy and seven beautiful grandchildren: Doron, Limore, Michael, Allon,

Adi, Shira, and Adam. I am now also a great grandfather of six thus far: Noa, Talia, Evan, Gabriella, Emily and Lev!

Sixty years ago, if someone had told me that this is how my life would turn out, I would never have believed it! I never thought it would turn out so well. I always imagined the worst – not death but of a hard life. It turned out so very well. I have a beautiful family, a house, a condominium in Florida and a successful business. I feel I want for nothing. If I would have to live over my life again, I probably wouldn't do it any differently. It wasn't enough to just be smart to survive the Holocaust. Being smart didn't change anything, one couldn't figure out anything. There was no way to pre-determine, to know what was going to happen; I must have survived because it was destined.

Always, I hoped that I would find someone close to me from my life before the war – my brother, my aunts, uncles, someone, but they were all murdered. Many are completely unaccounted for and I am the only survivor to bear witness for my family.

In the beginning, I could not speak of my experiences. Then, when I spoke of the atrocities I witnessed, people would turn away in disbelief, so I said nothing or very little.

The first time I truly spoke was during a trip to Poland for the 50th anniversary of the Warsaw Ghetto Uprising. En route to Auschwitz, I found myself on a bus filled with survivors and delegates of the Jewish Congress from Toronto. The leader of the group asked if anybody wanted to say something. Elaine, my wife, encouraged me, she said, "Get up there!" After speaking, as I returned to my seat, Anita Eckstein, a member of Holocaust Centre of Toronto, stopped me. She told me, "Henry, we need people like you to speak." This opened the floodgates for me to express my personal testimonial of survival.

I now spend much of my time volunteering, educating, and lecturing students at universities, high schools through the Holocaust Education Centre across Toronto, its suburbs and in the United States in the Miami area of Florida.

Not a day goes by that I do not think about my family and reflect about the horrors I witnessed throughout the holocaust. All I can ask, now that my story has been shared, is to **never forget!**

Afterward

In the words of the many who love and have learned much from Henry:

Henry has survived unimaginable terror, and he has come away from his pain to bear witness, to share his story, his wisdom and his unimaginable loss, an enormous void for all the Jewish people and for all of humankind. He is cherished by those whose lives he has touched: family, step-family, the huge number of children who affectionately call him Saba (grandfather in Hebrew), and have shared, learned so much, and grown through his love! An extraordinary human being, having lost absolutely everything, Henry rebuilt his world to include tolerance, understanding and tremendous love.

Praying for his survival, his mother forced him forward. Against all odds, with strength, determination and with tremendous good fortune, Henry survived, and did exactly as his mother once prayed he would. He stayed alive to tell his harrowing and horrifying experience and to share his family with his audience. This is an account of loss and of redemption, of chance and of acceptance. The success, the love, and the nachas[41] of his children and their children remain forever his living testament!

His story lives on through the thousands of students of varying races, ethnic backgrounds, and religions who have felt the impact of his words and learned his message of tolerance. Let the Holocaust never be repeated and let Henry's words never be forgotten.

---

[41] Joy, blessings and sense of pride.

Appendix

Map of Henry's Movements

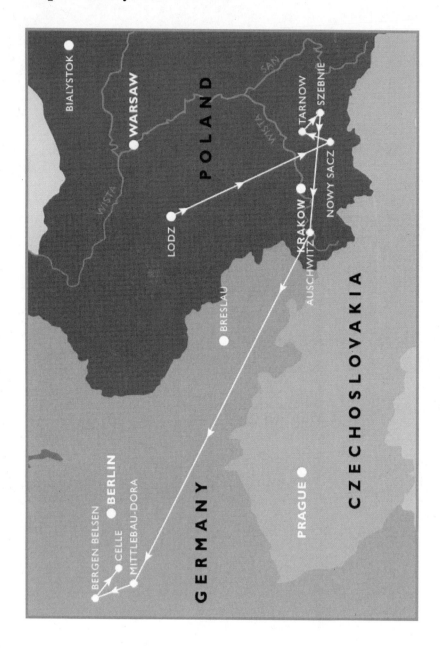

By My Mother's Hand

Timeline of Henry's Experiences

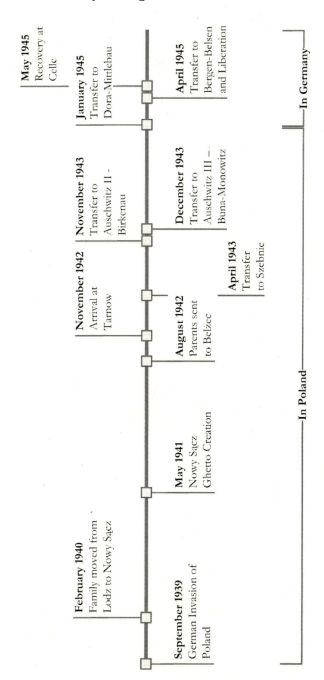

Henry Melnick

Henry's Pre-War Family Tree

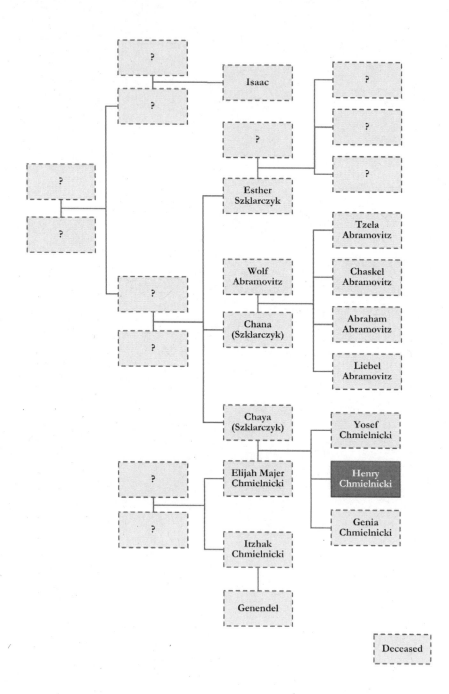

Henry's Post-War Family Tree

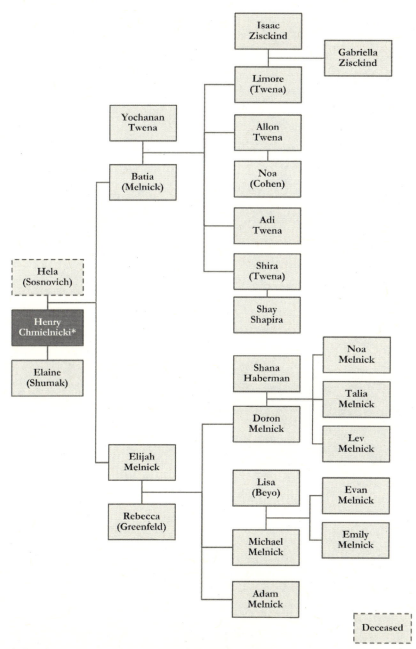

*Chmielnicki was changed to Melnick in 1974

Henry's Immediate Family's Details

Mother: Chaya (Szklarczyk) Chmielnicki*
Born: December 24th 1890, Radomsko, Poland
Died: August 24th 1942, Bełżec, Poland

Father: Eliyahu Majer Chmielnicki*
Born: April 1888, Rozprza, Poland
Died: August 25th 1942, Bełżec, Poland

Son: Elijah Chmielnicki* (Eli Melnick)
Born: September 17th 1948, Tel Aviv, Israel

Daughter: Batia Chmielnicki* (Betty Twena)
Born: June 16th, 1953, Tel Aviv, Israel

* **Chmielnicki was changed to Melnick in 1974**

By My Mother's Hand

Hela's Family Tree

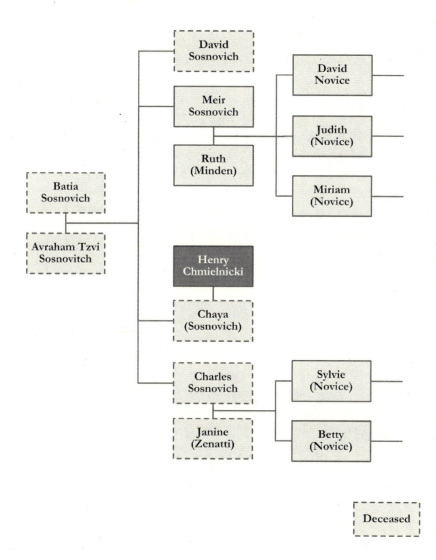

Modern-Day Photographs

Henry Melnick, October 2009

Henry and Elaine (Shumak) Melnick, May 2010

Henry in front of Start Auto Electric in Toronto, July 2010

Henry leading a Holocaust education session in Bal Harbor, Florida, January 2011

By My Mother's Hand

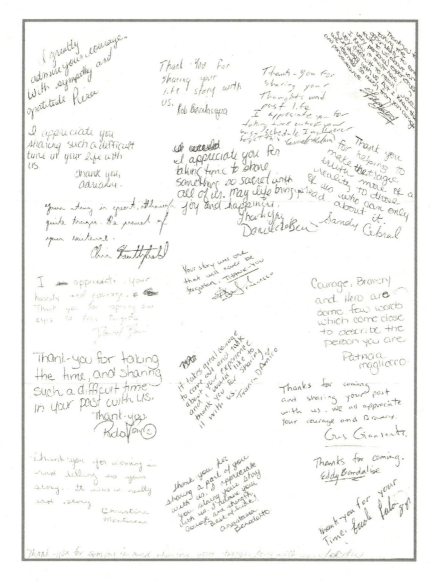

Various students' written comments after listening to Henry speak

205

Henry's son Elijah (Eli) and wife Rivka Melnick

Rivka & Eli's sons Michael, Adam and Doron Melnick

Talia, Noa, Lev, Doron and Shana Haberman

Michael, Lisa (Beyo), Emily and Evan Melnick

Henry's daughter Batia and husband Yochanan Twena

Betty & Yochanan's children Adi, Limore, Shira and Allon

Isaac Zisckind, Limore (Twena), and Gabriella

Noa (Cohen) and Allon Twena

Shay and Shira (Twena) Shapira

Henry with six of his seven grandchildren and
five of his six great grandchildren, November 2010.
Not pictured: Lev, Shira and Shay